50 POSTS AND A

PIECE OF TOAST

RODNEY JOHNSON

ISBN 978-1547120475

Printed in the United States of America
Cover design: Galan*Graphix*

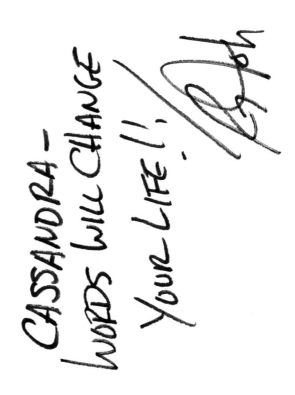

CASSANDRA -
WORDS WILL CHANGE
YOUR LIFE!!

Contact Information

Comedy Bookings: Call Rodney Johnson at 404.427.1056. comedianrj@aol.com (That's right. AOL.)

Motivational Speaking and Lectures: Call Kelly Cole, Prime Time Marketing at 276.591.7427.

College Appearances: Call Brian Dennis, Diversity Talent Agency at 404.539.3934.

Dedication

This book is dedicated to a multitude of people for various reasons. First to my children, they're the ones I got up every morning for, trying my best to be a responsible father and provider by teaching them to make solid choices to produce a successful life. While I tried to teach them the lessons I've learned, you'll have to ask them what I brought to their lives. I sincerely wanted them to know the love of a father, to enjoy life on their own terms and build upon the foundation I laid. I understood that each day would bring different challenges, but I wanted them to know how to prevail through adversity. This book is a testament to their courage, commitment and desire to make the best choices for themselves. I can say with pride that my children can stand on their own two feet and are constantly trying to make their lives better. I don't always agree with their choices, but I respect them. This book was written with them on my heart as I carry them with every step I take. I thank God for allowing me to stand in the gap and guide the lives of Travis, Cierra, Natalie, Marcus, and Janai. Enjoy the journey!

I would also like to dedicate this book to Jerry Broadnax. Jerry is the only manager I ever had. He was the first person that saw my talent and signed me to his agency after my first performance. He was a father figure to me in my early days of learning my craft. I had talent, but it was unpolished. He took the time to guide me and opened the doors that led to the career I have today. As a former NFL player, he knew I needed to put in the work to be successful. Jerry would take me to every open mic night across Dallas. He was persistent with getting me on shows with top artists of the day. I opened shows for The Rose Brothers, Paula Abdul, Shalamar, DeBarge, and even New Kids on the Block. Jerry would always stand in the wings, beaming with pride. Even when I got booed off the stage, he would find one nugget I could use for the next time. He was not only my manager, but also a friend. Thank you Mr. Broadnax, your influence helped shape me into the man I am today.

Then there's Angel Carter, Nancy Pettaway, Allie Faye Jones and Beverly Metoyer. These ladies spoke truth into my life at the darkest time. They are all my friends. I can't tell you how many late night emergency calls I put in to these women. With love, they all told me the truth. My emotions were all over the place but they didn't sugar coat anything. Sometimes we would laugh and other times they came at me hard. 'I know you're hurt but stand back up. Enough of the crying, what are you going to do now? OK, it's time to stop wallowing in pity. You're not a victim, you're a victorious survivor. You've failed but you'll get back up again.' These are the words they spoke to me time and time again. I remember asking when would the hurt subside, and they all said, 'in due time.' Through the pain I found my purpose. I knew what I was called to do. I've always been funny but I never had a message. My failed marriage and the strength of these women helped shape the next chapter not only in my life, but also in my career. Thank you ladies for all that you stood for and allowing God to use you to save me.

Table of Contents

Foreword

Rodney Johnson is a funny guy. Since his comedic talent was introduced on the Oprah Winfrey Show some 20 years ago, he has entertained audiences on television, cruise ships, college campuses, and in nightclubs and comedy stages across the nation and abroad. Rodney took to the comedy stage the lessons of his life experience as the son of a Baptist Minister, a Deacon in the Church, an Army Veteran, a husband, and a father. He has used his childhood escapades and the knocks and bangs of growing up as fodder for jokes that tickled the funny bones of diverse audiences. Viewing life through a God-centered lens, Rodney turned his lifelong connection to the church into a *Christian Comedy Tour*, bringing laughter to congregations around the country.

In *50 Posts and a Piece of Toast*, we meet a down-to-earth Rodney who is also purposely reflective, a seeker of knowledge, a man committed to family and church. He shares with the reader how he has been able to surmount his personal challenges with a "no excuse" approach to daily activities and a practical direction for achieving long-term goals. Rodney gives us a candid look at "what's important to me and at least what I *think* I know so far." In an easy read first book, he takes us along with him as he undertakes an honest and revealing discovery of self.

In sharing his life's journey with us, Rodney offers us some interesting nuggets and insights that may easily resonate. We see him consider the matters of everyday life and respond to God's grace in his married life, his child rearing, and his workaday world. This is one funny guy who always gives credit where credit is due, to God. Crediting his staying power to God's grace, he says,

> *"He carried me when I didn't know I needed to be carried, and I have landed on my feet. I fell, but by His grace, I'm still standing. By His mercy, I'm still able to be here learning and sharing the truth of the God I serve. God is the solution to your situation, and if he's not the solution, you have a serious situation."*

Dr. Julia Deborah Sterrett, President
Consultants in Human and Organizational Systems
Battle Creek, Michigan

Preface

About a month before I turned 50 years old, I decided to start writing about my life experiences on Facebook. Each day I wanted to post something that was important to me that helped shape my life. I wanted to post the 50 most important things I learned over the years every day, leading up to my 50th birthday. Fifty years is half of a century and you should have a story to share. God has kept me through countless, challenging situations. Through it all, I believe I've learned critical lessons on this journey—lessons worth sharing.

I strongly believe that we should all take time to reflect over the years we've been given. In doing so, we gain true perspective. Perspective is essential. It is often our perspective that dictates the shape of our path—past, present and future.

As a youth, I felt like I understood the meaning of life. I had an old-school spirit with a ton of wisdom at a young age, so I've been told. My father was a preacher and I'd not only listen to him preaching the sermon but I'd listen to the response of the church. We would talk about it on the drive home and he was always amazed about the small things I'd pick up—like if he should have closed earlier or if the congregation wasn't "with him."

I remember leaving a church service once, thinking it was a cult. I guess that was an easy call since some of the members were foaming at the mouth, but that's a story for another book.

To me, life has never been as complex and difficult as we make it out to be. Don't get me wrong, there are unseen hurdles to clear and rivers to cross, but our decisions, actions, and even inaction can further complicate our course.

I thought I knew about everything that involved me. I tried to always be on point and not have an excuse about anything. Every time I was asked a question, I had an answer. No matter what the question was, I had an answer. I felt like I was prepared for life. I had seen failure and I wasn't going to be a part of it nor would it ever be a part of me. How can you fail if you have an answer? Whenever I was interviewed, reporters would always tell me how complete my answers were. I wanted my answer to have substance and also give you something to think about.

I really thought I knew it *all*.

I was willing to provide for my family, take the lead, fix all of the problems, and even sacrifice my life to make the road as smooth as possible for those who followed my lead. I wanted to be counted on and trusted. I was Superman and I would swoop in, solve the problem and save the day. I wanted to be the HERO. There was never an option to surrender. There was no deterrent I could not overcome. I always found 'yes' in the middle of 'no.' I was built to succeed and come through; failure was not an option, and it certainly was not a part of my mindset. My thinking was critical and my mindset was bolted in determination. I could figure out how to get things done and make the process appear effortless. Situations were simple if you used common sense, which is not always found in a book. I've always looked to find the simplest road to achieve the maximum reward.

When it came to wealth, I envisioned multiple streams of income to increase my family's well-being and brought them to fruition. I listened to people who were smarter than me, but then rearranged their philosophy to make it simple and easier for others to obtain. At this point you'll notice I've used a lot of 'I,' 'I,' and 'I.' It's important to let you know that all of my thinking was centered around 'I.' In my mind, it was for those I loved, but I was going to make it all happen. I believed I had all the answers and if you looked at my lifestyle, you may have agreed. Some preachers I knew told me they were covetous over the cars I drove. I've owned cars from BMW, Lexus and Mercedes Benz. I knew some people were jealous and envious of the material things I obtained, but that never bothered me because I wasn't living for them. In my mind, I was ascending up my own ladder of success.

I wasn't trying to keep up with the Joneses, I was living for myself, and taking whoever I was responsible for along for the ride. I was trying live my life better than the life my parents gave me. They did the best they could and I wanted to take their best and do better. I was leaping off of their shoulders and before I landed, I already had a good view of where I needed to be in life. You don't grow up to go backwards. Slaves didn't escape from slavery for their children to be free and then return to bondage. It's called progression and I wanted my parents to be proud of their hard work.

Every day was filled with thinking and maneuvering to put myself in the best possible situation. Each move I made was to enhance my life and live above the rim. In my mind, everything was perfect.

Perfectly flawed, that is.

You see, I was oblivious to the needs of those around me because in my psyche, *I* had all the answers. Whatever you thought, I overruled that thought and made it better or at least I thought I was making it better. You couldn't possibly want what you asked for, so I would give you what you asked for, but a better version of your desire. Like if you wanted a four-cylinder car, I'd convince you, you needed a six-cylinder car because it had more power. I didn't hear the request of the people I loved because I was too busy trying not to fail, while failing. You can't see your failure while you're failing because you're actually living in the moment of your failure. When do you see the errors of your ways? When you're alone in the abyss of your own demise, everything becomes abundantly clear. When you wake up in an empty house and you hear your voice echoing in a place that was once filled with life, you get it.

While I was going through the 'I' process, God couldn't get my attention. He sent many messages, but I wasn't listening because I had all of the answers. He had my complete attention when everything I worked for was gone. My wife left me; the kids were living in other places;

17

the cars were repossessed; the house was in foreclosure; and for the first time in my life, I had no answer. I was at the bottom and had no clue how I got there or when was I going to resurface. Everything I thought I knew was turned upside down, reversed and spun out of control. I sat in the only thing left in my house, a La-Z-Boy chair. The house was motionless and no longer occupied by my family I labored for day after day, month after month, and year after year. I began to reflect on the prior 15 years of my life in my empty home, gazing out of the window.

For the first time in my life, I realized I did not know as much as I thought I knew. I no longer had the solution. I succumbed to the reality that my works were trumped by my own works. It seemed like I sat in my La-Z-Boy chair for days. My family was gone, my drive was depleted, and my desire to take another step in life had come to the end of the road.

I became a broken vessel.

I asked God why I couldn't get my family to understand that everything about me was based on providing for them. The battles, the endless travel, the long nights and the countless hours driving from gig to gig were solely for them. I did it all for them. The Holy Spirit's response knocked me to my knees: *How do you think Jesus felt? Look at everything He did, and they hung him on the cross! He died so that we might have life. He was blameless and yet he was blamed.*

I began to cry and ask for forgiveness. As I meditated on His answer, I was overcome with grief. Suddenly, scriptures and mantras I'd heard as a child flooded my mind—only what you do for Christ will last, I will look to the hills for my help, and sorrow may last for a little while, but joy comes in the morning. How do you think God felt about the treatment of His Son based on all that He did for us? Who am I in comparison to Jesus Christ, the living Savior? I was just a vessel He was using for his glory, but I wanted the praise for myself. I wanted people to see me and all that I was able to do. So He allowed people to treat me the same way we treat Jesus—disregarded and ignored.

I realized the accomplishments in my life were insignificant and of no consequence. I was mindful of the blessings from God, but still desired the praises that were exclusively His. I was arrogantly blessed, but too busy to acknowledge that my help came from Him. I should have been thankful for what God was allowing to happen in my life as well as the lives of those He entrusted in my care. Yet, it took my wife walking out of my life, my kids estranged and living apart, and an empty house for me to understand the depth of where I was and experience the utter majesty of God.

When you are in the bowels of your own sorrow, you can hear God's voice clearly. You become aware of the simplest things you once overlooked. I can attest that while at my lowest, I heard His voice and could finally see the error of my ways. I could see how many times He tried to get my attention. I was moving at warp speed and didn't have time to open up my ears and hear from Him. Experience teaches you not to repeat the same mistakes again. I hear more clearly now and I get out of the way and allow God to have His way in all things.

Even though I have not gotten it all right, I recognize that God has given me a certain amount of wisdom along this journey. I never intended to write a book. I started posting my thoughts on social media as a reflective exercise on things I have learned over the last 50 years. The feedback from various people was overwhelmingly clear—to put these thoughts in a book. Well, I have answered the call and I hope this book is a blessing.

You may agree or disagree with some of my reflections based upon your life experiences. You may take issue with some of my thoughts, wage a silent war with yourself, or you just might enjoy this book written by a comedian. You may laugh out loud and look around for someone to share that moment with. All I know is that I wanted to capture what's important to me and at least what I *think* I know so far. I will continue to stand for what I believe in and I know that God will keep teaching and guiding me because at this time in my life I am willing to listen to His instructions.

Thank you for supporting my first book and I hope you are blessed by something you read. I now realize it wasn't by my own efforts, but by God who kept me from the perils of my own wisdom. He carried me since I didn't know I needed to be carried and I have landed on my feet. I fell, but by his grace, I'm still standing. By his mercy I'm still able to be here learning and sharing the truth of the God I serve. God is the solution to your situation and if He's not the solution, you have a serious situation.

The Last $20

"There's nothing wrong with spending your last $20 on the person you love." I remember hearing this in church one Sunday morning from a guest speaker. Although he wasn't a preacher, he shared with us the things he learned from his father growing up. This quote stuck with me and for good reason. We spend much of our lives working to earn a decent income to provide for our families as well as ourselves. Most of what we make goes toward paying bills that we've created for things we wanted, but didn't necessarily need. Many people today are living check to check with little or no savings account. The average American has less than $500 in savings. While always trying to get ahead, we forget to take time to enjoy our loved ones and ourselves. Life becomes a race without a finish line we can see. When you live check to check, you don't plan because you're trying to keep up with what you weren't able to pay with last week's check. When you're in debt, it never leaves your mind. Debt has a way of creeping into your daily thought process. I wanted to be financially able to provide for my family without stress and expose my children to as many experiences as possible. I wanted them to have the option to go to and fro without limitation.

When money is not a concern, life has a different meaning. You're able to think clearer and make better choices. When we live above our means, the norm becomes work, and the exception begets quality time. Here is where we become feeble and start treading water just to stay afloat.

At some point, the quest to have it all became a game consumed with paying bills and juggling credit limits. My spending was out of control. Credit cards were my second line of fabricated income to back up my primary earnings. If I had spending ability on any card, I interpreted that as fluid cash available for withdrawal and I'd figure out how to pay it later.

Each month I'd sit down and figure out how to 'rob Peter to pay Paul.' It became my life. Take from over here to pay over there. I was manipulating the calendar as if I were able to buy days. Pay this bill on the first, pay that one before the late fee kicks in, and transfer the balance to a credit card or not pay a bill at all…. In actuality, all I was doing was moving debt from one place to the next without a penalty. I was a one-man juggling act and all the while my marriage and family were falling apart.

I wasn't there to be a part of the family. I was on the road working to pay for STUFF. Material things are nice, but when they supersede quality time, eventually you'll lose or someone will pay the price. I didn't take any moments to smell the roses or to see where the roses were planted. Seldom did I take the time to just enjoy my wife or the life my success had brought us. Every gig I took was based on what needed to be paid.

I was always in constant motion to fill in the next crack to keep my fabricated financial security in remission. I was in the midst of these thoughts when I heard the speaker say there's nothing wrong with spending your last $20 on the one you love. I became emotional as I realized I hadn't taken the time to do that. I was consumed with paying car notes, buying jewelry and things that have since evaporated from my life. I had spent money on the big things, but couldn't find $20 to enjoy the simple things that connect the lives of the people you love. I decided I would always take a moment to step away from the madness of survival and spend the last $20 with the one I love.

Take time to get away with the one you love. Enjoying an ice cream cone on a park bench will do wonders for a relationship. Noticing the beauty of a park as you walk with your loved one or driving on scenic highway with no particular destination are things you can do to make a relationship last forever. I started looking for things to do with my wife and I've never stopped. It doesn't have to be with your family. This $20 can be shared with anyone you have a relationship with. Have a cup of coffee with a neighbor. Eat a school lunch with your grandchild. These are just a few ideas on how to spend your last $20. Such moments are some of life's greatest rewards. In the end you'll realize that the $20 you spent will have lasting memories far greater than any bill you could ever pay. The bills will always be there but the moments you share are priceless.

Fear

Never allow fear to steal your greatness. Fear has kept many talented people from reaching the successful pinnacle of their existence. Every time I finished a chapter in my life, the next chapter held more intrigue and excitement for what was yet to come.

Fear has trapped and confined many people into working the same dead-end job to pay for a lifestyle that can barely make ends meet. Fear will keep you in a fruitless relationship while holding onto worthless ideas about life. We are forced to get up every day like robots. Punch in. Count the hours. Clock out. Repeat.

If you can remove fear from your choices, you'll see that the world is yours and that the unknown can be exciting. You just have to believe in yourself and never allow anyone or anything to stop you.

I never set out to be a comedian. I thought I was going to play professional football like all the other kids from my neighborhood. Sports seemed like the ticket to success and stardom. I briefly attended Central State University in Ohio to try out for the football team. However it only took one hit from a strong defensive player to know that football was not going to be my ticket to success. After my short-lived college experience, I made a promise to myself that if I ever discovered my true natural talent, I would cherish it.

Months later, after college, I found myself doing physical fitness training in the Army. I will attest that the military is a great place for young men to build a foundation, to uncover one's strengths or weaknesses, and to later decide which road to take in life. Three years later, I knew it was time to turn the page and move on to the next chapter.

As I approached the end of my enlistment, I recall my sergeant telling me I couldn't make it out in the real world and that I'd be back in the service within six months. I told him to hold on to that thought. I did my time, got my start and set out to see what was next for me in a world that had no ceiling. I went into the Army in 1984 with $38 in my pocket and wearing a coat my grandmother bought me. When I got out three years later, I had about $1,500, a car and furniture, but no place to lay my head. I was determined to create a better life for myself. The fear of not having a job set up didn't stop me from leaving the Army. I went in with $38 and left with $1,500. In my mind I was rich and couldn't fail.

One thing I knew at an early age was that the word 'no' did not affect me. It just meant to keep going until I reached 'yes.' So, I left Fort Hood, Texas in January 1987 and headed to Dallas to attend DeVry Institute of Electronics. It took four months to find and secure a job. I then turned my attention to enrolling in school for the fall semester. I worked a full-time job, along with a part-time job and was in the National Guard for one weekend a month.

One September evening I walked onto a stage and performed for the very first time. The roar of laughter from the audience hooked me and that is when I knew my life would never be the same. After that 10 minute comedy routine, I knew the 9-to-5 job had to go and comedy was my ticket to the life I often thought about. I was ready to quit my job that night, but my father told me not to give up my job for a pipe dream. I didn't even know what a pipe dream meant or where it came from. I just knew I was itching to explore my new horizon.

Becoming a comedian would afford me the opportunity to work for myself and set no limits on where I could go in life. I was all in and not looking in the rear view mirror. I decided not to allow anyone or anything to derail the direction I was going in my career. I spent the next 18 months working at every club that would allow me to get on stage, whether they paid me or not. I just wanted the experience. I knew putting in the work was going to open the doors I needed to be successful.

I was determined to quit my job, itching to hit the road and fulfill my purpose of making people laugh around the world. I was making $257 a week and after taxes, bringing home $187 with no benefits. That wasn't enough money for me to even consider staying. My manager wanted me to wait until I was established locally before I quit my job. I wasn't thinking local, I was thinking national. I was also thinking about international places to see and be heard. To be honest, I saw the vision, was ready to run and I didn't care in which direction. I knew I had to leave the job behind and chart a course towards independence. I couldn't wait. I needed to know for myself if I was good enough to make a living out of comedy.

Every day I was looking for a reason to quit my job. The thought of taking a risk was like a drug. From the moment I told myself I wanted to be a comedian, going to work was becoming more difficult. I was always on edge, looking for a reason to say, "I'm out." In my mind I could see all that I wanted to do and achieve. The door opened for me one winter morning in 1988 when I asked my supervisor to inspect some multi-wired circuit boards that I needed to pass in order to move to the next phase. He told me the process was not complete and to call him in two hours for another inspection. I was joking when I said, "When I become supervisor, I will pass these along." He looked me straight in my eyes and didn't blink or crack a smile and stated the following:

"Supervisor? You'll never be a supervisor here. There's no room for advancement for you here."

Talk about being shocked and stunned! I placed the board back into the process and sat down to write my letter of resignation. In my mind there was no reason for me to stay another day. You're telling me I'll only be a worker and nothing more. I believed I had too much talent to work for a three percent pay raise once a year. After completing my handwritten letter of resignation with misspelled words and no punctuation, I walked down to the human resources office to submit it. The HR director looked it over and said these infamous words:

"We will not rescind this."

They were telling me that if I changed my mind, they would not take me back, but for me there was no going back. Once you become fearless, your choice of words becomes bold and self-assured.

"I didn't put it in to be rescinded," I replied. "I'll never work here again, or any other job. I'm going to pursue comedy and see where that road takes me."

I also got on the loud speaker and told the entire company I'd never come back there to work. A good friend told me to never say 'never.' She was afraid that I'd need that job down the road. I assured her I was never going back, and I never did—except for that one time I visited in my Cadillac....

The realization that I had no chance for advancement was the push I needed that gave me the courage to quit and walk away from the workforce. I had the freedom to make my own way and not depend on working for others at a fraction of the cost. I wanted to become the CEO of my own company and create wealth for my family. I wanted to live without restrictions and never be restricted to a 15-minute break again.

You have to trust your own ability if you want to defeat fear. I knew I was funny, but I had to put in the work to be successful. It's not just going to come to you. I always told my children that everyone fits into one of three categories: You're an employee, a manager, or the owner. To be the owner, you have to be willing to take the risk.

Fear is a mindset, but the body can prevail by moving forward in the direction of the thing you fear.

Fear is a thought that movement can erase. Fear is a mindset. I said it again just in case you missed it the first time. You have to think positive to have positive results. I knew what I was going to do with my life and as long as I knew that, I didn't have to worry. Everything would revolve around performing. If it didn't involve entertainment, then I had no need to do it. Sometimes we become a jack of all trades and a master of none. I didn't want to spread myself thin by trying to be a comedian-teacher-plumber just to make ends meet. Whatever you do to pay your bills, that's what you are. I wasn't afraid to leave the Army and I wasn't afraid to leave my 9 to 5 stranglehold job. The owner of the company never knew my name. I was just a person that worked for him with a payroll number. You can give your life to a job and they'll hire someone to replace you moments after the funeral. Don't be afraid to explore your greatness. If you feel you don't have any greatness then set your alarm clock for the morning. One day, you'll wake up.

Real Men Cry

There's nothing wrong with crying. Even Jesus wept (John 11:35). I've always enjoyed a good cry. Crying helps release your emotions. 'Real men don't cry' is a saying I heard many times while growing up. I disagree. Real men cry when they're overwhelmed and are truthful with their feelings. I've cried wherever, in front of whomever, and whenever the moment has prompted me to release my built-up anguish and pain.

Crying is like rain, it lasts for a little while, but after a good rain, the sun will shine to rejuvenate the earth. Crying will release those feelings that you've kept locked up on the inside. I believe if men cried more, they'd live longer. Men seldom talk about the issues that plague them. That keeps a lot of men feeling trapped on the inside with no place to release that strain. We die of stress and heart-related problems because we think showing emotion isn't manly. Well you hold on to that, I'm going to shed a few tears and live a few extra years.

My favorite crying movies are, *The Pursuit of Happyness*, *Coach Carter*, and *Patch Adams*. Every time I watch those movies, I shed a few tears. There is just something about the resilience of the human spirit that moves me to tears. Whenever I see a father taking the time to spend quality time with his family, I'm moved. The father is the head of the household and his leadership is needed if we are going to save our communities. Strong men embrace challenges that sometimes require them to steal away to cry. It is presumed as a weakness should a man cry, but I've found strength in connecting with my most sincere and heartfelt emotions. In these movies, the lead male character had to cry a few times. They cried to get through the situation of being overwhelmed by the magnitude of life. No matter the reason, they cried and prevailed.

If Jesus wept, then why can't I?

A Song in your Heart

Have a song in your heart that you can leave on repeat. You need a song that feeds you. My song is, *Love's In Need of Love Today* by Stevie Wonder. The lyrics of a song can be the blueprint for your life. When I hear this song, I know that the world is missing love. So many things are going on today that if we could just stop and embrace the moment, we'd see that love is missing. Some children are three sentences away from killing you or falling into your arms looking for love.

Music has connected people throughout the world. We've found solace and consolation in music. How many times have you heard a song and it took your mind back to a certain place or time? Like the first time you slow danced with the person you would spend the rest of your life with. When you get married there's always a first dance to a song that defines your feelings for one another. When life sends us trial after trial and you don't think you can take another disappointment, you should have a song that gives you strength and lets you know you can overcome any adversity.

I love songs that connect to real life. The words move you and take you on a journey. Find your song and share it with those you meet along the way. Music changes lives and connects souls.

Be on Time

When it comes to time, early is great, on time is acceptable and late comes with excuses. As a child, I often heard that the early bird catches the worm. I've benefited in so many ways from being on time. I've been early to airports and was able to get on an earlier flight before a storm approached. Punctuality makes me dependable, Trust me, people notice. When you're late, you're telling the person waiting on you that it's ALL about you. We've all sat in the doctor's office waiting for our name to be called. Time passes as you wait with an attitude. If being on time isn't important, then why would you sit there looking at your watch and stating how long you've been waiting to be seen? It's about the doctor, not your health issue. When you're late, you're saying, 'I'll arrive when I can and you'll wait until I get there.'

There is no excuse when you have ample time to make the appointment or meeting. Promptness is a habit for me— a way of life. How can you be late to work when you knew before you left you had to be back at the same time the next day? People who are late make excuses all the time for being late. Tardiness is a process of not understanding the concept of time and how to apply it evenly. You may only live 15 minutes from your job, but if you don't factor in traffic, inclement weather or accidents and collisions, you'll be late before you even leave the house. Being on time is also about putting your priorities in order. What's important is determined by your ability to get there on time. I understand there are circumstances that will arise which can alter your schedule. There are occurrences that are beyond your control for instance, an accident, your car breaking down or a sudden health issue. Late people—you know who you are and we know who you are—you'll be late to your own funeral. I guess that's the best time to be late.

Time is always moving forward and once it passes you can never get it back. What you can do is enjoy being on time to have more time to be a part of whatever is going on. It's a valuable habit to possess; it provides a level of confidence and trust. My children know I'm always on time. It makes me dependable and even if they never tell me, I know it matters to them because they matter to me.

Don't agree? After all that I said, I know some of you will continue in your folly because it's all about you. Here's the final nail in the coffin... if being on time isn't important, why do people always apologize when they're late? You must agree with that. My time has run out on this chapter.

Hurt vs. Regret

Have you ever been hurt? Think about how you felt when your first love came to an abrupt end and in that moment you believed you would never live to see another day without that person. Hurt has a way of healing itself in due time. If you fall and scrape your knee, in time it will heal. I've learned over the years that time does heal all wounds, but regret lives forever. Regret has lingering side effects beyond hurt and it doesn't seem to ever go away.

After my failed marriage, I was hurt and didn't know how long I would have to deal with the pain. In due time, the hurt lessened and the healing began. Make no mistake, I was definitely heartbroken that my marriage was over, but I had no regrets. What is regret? I believe it's when you didn't put in the necessary effort to build a strong relationship, maximize the time that was given and quit without really trying to resolve your issues. Maybe it was pride, envy or plain old selfishness, but down the road you'll realize you made a mistake—a mistake that could have easily been fixed with a simple 'I'm sorry, please forgive me or let's work this out together.' If you choose to listen to the misguided advice of others instead of apologizing, you'll have many regrets, and those who tried to give you wise counsel will have gone on with their lives.

I've tried to live my life without regrets. Relationships that are important should always have first priority and get your time and attention. Regret is a thought that creeps into your mind periodically. It doesn't hurt like it did at first, but still requires you to think about and tend to it. Just when you think you have healed, something comes up to remind you of what you once had.

Here's a story about regret. I have a friend who was married for 10 years. Her husband adored her and was truly in love with being a husband and a friend. In the middle of the night she would have a desire for ice cream. He would ask her what flavor, get up and go to the store. Never did he complain about taking care of her needs and wants. He worked hard and was respected by her family. He was just a good man. She always complained about him being boring and a homebody. On her job she met a guy that was fun and always doing something that she found interesting. Instead of sharing this with her husband, she began to hang out with her co-worker. You know how the story goes. She leaves her husband for the shiny new toy. After her divorce, she moves in with the fun guy. The guy on the job is the worst guy to be with. He never really gets to know you and you don't know him. You just enjoy the excitement he brings and he likes not being responsible for you. He gets all the answers because you tell him everything that's going on in your relationship. You should be at home working to save the relationship you already have. After several months together, the real dude shows up. He didn't pay his bills on time and her mother didn't like him. One night she said she wanted some ice cream. He said, "Me too." She has lived with regret ever since. If you mention his name, she'll say, "I don't know what I was thinking." My only point is to do all you can while you can so that if it doesn't work out, you have no regrets.

You may be able to move on and even talk about past hurt, but regret sometimes is a daily thought you just can't get over. That's why when I'm in a relationship of any sort, I'll give my all, so that I don't have to look back and wish I would have done something different. From friendships to marriages, I've tried to be accountable. If for some reason a relationship ended, I didn't want to look back and have remorse or guilt.

Hindsight is 20/20 and some say you can always do something differently to change the outcome of your situation. I agree and I choose to do it all while I'm in the moment. My only regret was having two children with two different women. I don't regret that they were born. I just regret not raising them full time. I love my kids, but I'd have preferred to raise them and be a part of their life every waking morning. They both know how much I love them and I have never tried to avoid the responsibilities of being their father. It would have been nice to see them grow through each stage of their lives under my roof instead of watching from a bird's eye view. No matter how much child support you pay, nothing is like being in the home raising your children. I live with that and each day I work to make sure my kids know how much they mean to me.

Small Things

I've always believed that small things matter. My agent often said, "Don't sweat the small stuff." To me, small things collectively build a greater picture. Just think of the masterpieces we miss when we don't take time to collect the minute pieces.

Counting pennies may seem small, but those coins will tally up into an account over time and can possibly supplement your retirement.

Small things matter. I've never been too busy to talk to people who attended my shows. Whenever I finished a performance, I was determined to be the last person to leave. I can't tell you how many extra DVDs I sold or how many referrals I acquired to perform at other places simply because I paid attention and focused on the small things. Sometimes it was a handshake or smile, and other times it was simply taking the time to listen and hear another person's philosophy, sentiments and views.

Sometimes, it's the smallest gesture that captures a person's heart, and they will remember that moment forever. Remember the widow in the Bible who put two small copper coins in the offering plate at the temple? Her offering was the smallest, but the most memorable because she gave all she had.

Small things add up to the essence of life.

Experience is the Best Teacher

My favorite line over the last several years has been: experience is the best teacher. We've all heard that saying at some point in time, right? I wanted to give it more meaning, so I added: why experience it, if you have a teacher? In other words, listen and try to avoid the pitfalls that others have already fallen into. Why go through the same madness if you have a person willing to share their experience with you and help you navigate the crossroads of life?

Cease the generational curses, stop blaming what you lack on the past generation, stop playing the victim and begin to implement the wisdom that's being shared with you.

How many single mothers need to share their experiences before the next young girl listens and becomes a wife and not a baby mama? When will we listen to the stories of those who've ruined their credit before we understand how to live debt free and value a solid credit rating? Why wallow in failure when success is a matter of listening and applying solid, experienced information?

My father used to say he was a mathematical genius because he could make ends meet with a limited amount of money. He took pride in figuring out how to pay three bills with one dollar and a chicken wing. It was a circus and he was the ringmaster. He'd always made enough money to pay his bills, but found intrigue in devising schemes to help someone else out of their demise. It was a game he truly enjoyed to the end. He never was a planner, he was a reactor. I inherited his fiscal footsteps of wheeling and dealing. One day I asked my agent why he never complained about money and his reply changed my entire life. He said, "Make more and spend less." That statement changed my life and saved it as well.

Why do we live above our means and then spend the rest of our lives trying to get out of the debt we created? We create debt largely due to excessive wants. In most cases, our needs are taken care of, but we use credit cards for wants and borrow money to pay for our needs. Then we find ourselves in a stressful debt situation which pressures us to keep looking for a way out. Yet we keep adding more wants on top of what we already can't afford, that in most cases, we don't even need. We tend to think our wants validate and makes us feel important. Keep trying to keep up and you'll continue to be one step behind those that really don't matter.

Listen to those who've already been down the road you're traveling. It didn't take a rocket scientist for me to understand I didn't need to fall into certain traps of the comedy business in order to succeed. I listened to the comedians who were in the game before me and they allowed me to stand on their shoulders to get a good view of the roads I needed to take in order to become successful. My goal was to never work a day job again. I listened. I heard those who spoke and I applied the information they

41

shared. I was told to open a retirement account at age 27, so I did. Now, as I near retirement age, I'm in good shape to come off the road and retire.

I didn't get everything right and I wish I had listened to more of the advice others shared over the years. Yet if I chose not to listen, I never blamed anyone but myself. If I was in a situation that could have been avoided, I just kept moving and fought my way out. I didn't blame anyone for the outcome. I stood up and took responsibility for not listening to the experienced teachers I had in my life. If you have a teacher that's trying to help you, please listen and if all possible, avoid the road that leads to circumstances that may cause regret later in life.

For some crazy reason with all that we hear, we still end up going through the experience anyway and then we try to warn the next person. They won't listen either, just like you.

Make it a point to embrace the words of the wise and you'll have a greater chance of living a rewarding life. Experience is the best teacher and it will teach you the easy way or the hard way. Either way, you'll learn.

"No."

Hearing 'no' when it comes to business dealings or providing for my family has never discouraged me. Early in my career, I heard the word 'no' frequently and often, but fortunately I was chastised with an explanation. 'No,' he's not ready, he needs more time to develop or just plain 'no,' we don't think he's right for our club. When I heard 'no,' I realized that I wasn't getting the job at that moment in my amateur career. Men cannot allow that word to dictate their outcome. 'No' means that it's time to figure out something else or choose a new approach. Hearing this word builds character, cognitive reasoning skills and faith. No matter how many times I heard that word, in my heart I know that in the end, I'd prevail. 'No' is not a means to stop, but to begin anew— especially if you believe in what you're doing.

In life there are different roads to take and each one will lead you to a destination, but each one contains obstacles you'll have to overcome. 'Yes' is always easier. We often wish all answers could be 'yes,' but I believe the best stories come from 'no.' I auditioned for Star Search in 1987. I was told I wasn't ready for the show. I was performing at the Improv in New York City in 1991. An executive producer was in the audience that night and offered me a spot to appear on Star Search in 1992. Four years later, I earned my 'yes.' It can be discouraging when you continue to hear 'no,' but always remember that persistence and focus defeats the infamous word. Remember, a delay does not mean a denial. 'No' may just mean that it's not time.

Don't let this tiny word stop you from your quest. It can only make you more confident and self-assured. When you finally conquer the task at hand, you'll look back and realize 'no' was just a test to see you if you would go forward or retreat. Seize your greatness. When you can handle the word 'no,' you'll appreciate the word 'yes.'

Street Lights

I thank God for street lights. I had to be home by the time they came on. My father would tell us, "Your butt better be in front of this house when that light comes on." We could play all day. It seemed like I was never tired. From playing hide-and-go-seek to freeze tag, we were always on the move. The neighborhood was full of life and to this day I still laugh at the games we made up. You always knew when your time of ripping and running the streets with your friends was about to come to an end for the day. Like all good things, the day would come to an end and we all had the same indicator, the street light.

First, there was a sound of electricity going through the post and then the light would start to flicker. Once it was bright you better be in the house or in front of it. If not, the next thing you heard was friends telling you that your father was looking for you. Once you heard that, your heart started to race because you knew what was next. In retrospect, streets light saved my life. This concept provided the structure I needed as a child and helped me develop the tools I needed to become an adult. First, it taught me to be on time. It also taught me how to listen and follow instructions. These are the foundation blocks we all need to become productive adults. When I look back over my childhood, I realized that most of the kids in my neighborhood that had to be home before the street light came on turned out pretty well. The kids who could hang out all night and never had to go home are still hanging out to this day. And trust me when I tell you, it seemed like the kids that never had to go home had the most fun. I wanted to hang out all night just once to see what it felt like. I did test my dad a couple times and the results were not worth hanging out. It's no surprise how some of their lives turned out. Some went to jail and some died before every reaching the age of 30. Be grateful the next time you look at a street light if you lived by the code of being home before they came on.

No Excuses

My aunt taught me a valuable lesson many years ago. She would clearly articulate, "When I ask you to do something, the answer is yes I can or no I can't. I don't want to hear your explanation if you're unable to help or contribute."

I learned very early in life not to make excuses. Either you will or you won't. In the Army, I learned that the maximum effective range of an excuse is zero meters. Civilian translation? No one cares about your excuse, just get the job done or let someone else take the lead.

Ladies, if a man gives you a bunch of excuses about his inability to get a job, cut your losses and move on. Men need to stand behind the words that come out of their mouths or they need to keep their mouths shut. Real men don't make excuses. Men must do their best to live up to the expectations of those depending on them. If I said "I got it," then you can be rest assured it will be done. Some men are unreliable and make excuses to cover up their inability to be responsible. Men, if you ever want to reclaim your rightful role, stand up and be accountable for the words you release into the atmosphere.

Excuses are an easy way of getting out of not doing what you were supposed to do, and makes you look weak and ineffective in the eyes of the listener. Whenever someone gives us an excuse, we seldom tell that person we know they're just making excuses. Then we proceed to tell a third person the excuse we just heard to hear their reaction to what we already know. It comes down to thinking before you respond. How many of us really think before we speak? Very few, which leaves us with hearing tons of excuses as to why things didn't work out. Either you will or you won't, but keep your excuses to yourself. The world doesn't need to know how sorry you are, your actions have already told us the real story.

Loaning Money

Never loan money to people who you discern may not be able to pay you back. First, I don't believe in loaning people money. I believe in helping a person when I can. That means giving them what I can for that particular situation. When people have a need, they will borrow with good intentions. They'll even sound sincere about returning your money, but at the end of the day, you might be disappointed. Relationships, friendships and business partnerships have come to bitter ends over unpaid loans.

Sometimes you can get out of loaning someone money by asking questions. If you ask three questions, most people will say never mind after the second one. I bet you want to know the three questions. There's no correct line of questions that you could ask. Make them up. I've used the following: Who else knows about your situation? How did you get into this situation in the first place? Give me the information for the bill so I can make a payment for you. I know the last one wasn't a question, but it will put an end to the conversation. If you do happen to loan a person some money, never loan them an amount that you can't afford to lose.

I keep it simple. If I have extra money, I'll just bless them with what I have to help them out. Here's a little formula I use to ensure I never lose a family member or friend over money. If a person wants to borrow $500, I automatically divide that amount by four and I'll give them $125. When people ask to borrow money, they seem to always ask for more than what they need and an amount they might not be able to pay back. Ask Visa.

If someone owes you money, you hate to see that person wearing new clothes, taking a vacation or buying anything new knowing they owe you. People will even try to make you feel bad about returning the money they borrowed. Some borrowers have the audacity to bring up the possessions you have, such as the car you drive or the house you live in, as if those are valid reasons not to return your money. Having those belongings should be the number one reason to return the money. In the end, it's up to you. Do you want to be a blessing or would you rather be stressing? I prefer to bless, not to stress.

"It's hard, but it's fair."

My high school coach always used to tell us, "It's hard, but it's fair." I never understood what he was saying back then, but over time, it became clear as day. I was doing wind sprints when I'd hear him saying that phrase over and over again. In time, it became apparent that he was instilling a work ethic in us. Yes it's hard, but if you put in the effort now, in the end, it will be fair.

Life is like that.

You get out of life what you put into it. You reap what you sow. I put in the work and continued to move forward each day pressing toward my goals. I strive to improve in all areas of my life. There were some hard days and long nights of uncertainty, but my coach's words have always echoed in my head. In my mind I could still see that little smile on his face as he spoke and blew his whistle. I knew with hard work, my dreams would become reality.

Life's not fair at times, but it can be enjoyable when you understand what's necessary to live life at its zenith. Some days the road will be hard, but you have to learn how to maneuver around obstacles if you want to be successful. The fairness comes once you've laid the foundation of a solid effort.

You must prepare yourself for the race of life. No marathon runner just enters the race. They put in countless hours of training. They know they must eat right, rest, and allow time for healing. If they follow all the steps they'll be able to compete at the highest level and finish the race. No one owes you anything. If you get a helping hand up, be thankful for it and keep moving. It's hard to hit a moving target. Keep putting in the work, you'll reach your goal and be able to share the journey with others. Life is hard, but it's fair if you put in the work. I remember the wind sprints and they didn't kill me—they made me stronger.

Defining Moments

I think every person has defining moments that affect the outcome of their life and future. I've had several such moments and still lean on the lessons from them. When I was a child, I wanted to play little league baseball so I asked my dad if I could play and his response was 'yes.' I was excited, told all my friends I was going to play ball on an actual baseball field, as opposed to a parking lot using abandoned cars as bases.

There were three dates to sign up.

As the first date to sign up approached I asked my dad for the $19 I needed to be a part of the team. He said he didn't have it. I wondered why he didn't have the money because he worked every day. It made no sense to me. The second opportunity came for me to sign up and he forgot about it. I couldn't understand how he forgot, especially since I reminded him for weeks. On my third and final chance to sign up, he was drunk. My mother ended up taking me to sign up after she came home from work that evening.

On that very day I told myself from then on I would only depend on me. Never again would I allow anyone to disappoint me. From that day forward, I did whatever it took to have the money for the things I desired. I cut grass, bagged groceries at the market, sold freeze cups, had parties, raked leaves, and shoveled snow. One time I even thought about breaking into a house. It was just a thought, thank God. This moment in my life built character. It also made me dependable. I never wanted to go without for myself.

My next defining moment came during a thunderstorm. I was probably about 12 years old and was hanging out at the local shopping center. Out of nowhere a storm approached and fear kicked in. We lived about four blocks from the shopping center and with the high winds and heavy rain I knew I couldn't get home without being drenched. I knew my dad was home so I went to the pay phone to call him to come pick me up. I remember phone calls were 25 cents back then. I put the quarter in and called my dad. He answered the phone and I asked him to come pick me up due to the storm. A few seconds later the phone went dead. I thought the storm had knocked out our phone service so I called him again. Again he answered but this time he said "I'm not coming to get you" and hung up. Why would he not come and get his son? I was 12 years old, scared and the storm was in rare force. It was raining cats and dogs, like the old folks used to say. I went to the end of the shopping center and looked up the street. It was dark, the wind was blowing and the trees were swaying. It was eerie. After a few minutes I saw a break in the clouds and I took off running towards home. I ran for what seemed like dear life. When I got home I was out of breath and wet from head to toe. My dad was in the kitchen when I arrived. I didn't know what to expect and I wasn't about to speak to the man that wouldn't come get me. I didn't have to say much because he said it all. He looked at me and said "You made it," and walked away. Nothing else was ever said. Years later this is what I got from that experience: he was teaching me to become a man. We need to learn how to get home by any means necessary. We are built to keep moving through all situations. It's not going to be comfortable for us all the time. Yes, I got home that day and I've been coming home ever since. Nothing stops a man from his job to lead, provide and protect. I received that message loud and clear.

The last defining moment came while I was serving in the Army. As a private with a family, I didn't make much money. I was told I could qualify for food stamps since I had two dependents. I went to the Department of Social Services to apply for benefits. I had to stand in a long line with other applicants. After what seemed like hours, I reached the woman behind the window and was told I was in the wrong line. She sent me to the correct line and I started waiting all over again. I guess the thought of asking for help just wasn't a part of my nature. The longer I waited, the more I wanted to leave, but, as a solider I was entitled to the assistance or so I thought.

Once I got to the front of the line I was given a few forms to fill out. Just the thought of answering the questions made me want to walk out again, but I had a family and getting the extra help would make life a little easier until I was promoted. Upon completing the forms I had to stand in another line to turn them in. For some reason, I thought the decision would be immediate since I really needed the help. I was told that an answer would come within two weeks. I still had to wait to see if I was approved. After jumping through all the lines and filling out the paperwork, I received a letter stating I didn't qualify because I made $17 too much. I took my letter, went back to the Department of Social Services and told the supervisor I would never again apply for social or government funded programs to feed my family. I needed to provide for my family and was determined to make my own way. To fill in the void, I was a soldier by day and delivered pizzas at night. By any means necessary, I was going to make ends meet. I'd work from 6 a.m. to 5 p.m. and then deliver pizzas from 6 p.m. to about midnight. One night I was robbed. Two guys pulled out a shotgun to take my pizza. I wasn't harmed, but I was scared to death. That night I filled out a police report at the station and a lost report for the pizza. The next night, I was back in my car delivering pizzas. No robbery was going to stop me from I had to do. Provide. I've since realized that you'll never let yourself down. We may let down others, but when was the last time you failed yourself? I've learned to trust God. I took control of my choices and I played the hand that was dealt to me. I endured through it all. I knew my capabilities and failure was never an option.

My wife lying next to me and standing by my side was all the motivation I needed. Looking into my children's faces fueled my fight every day. I may not know what the future holds, but I've learned from the past and continue to press on for a better tomorrow.

Life Lessons Abound

You can learn something from everyone you meet. Everybody has a story to tell or an experience to share. From the homeless, to the CEO of a major company, you might just be amazed by the information they have to offer.

I remember one cold night I was working a club in DC. I had on corduroy pants, a sweater, and a winter coat. I was still cold. As I approached the club I noticed a homeless man trying to bum a cigarette from some people as they passed by him. When I approached, I told him I didn't smoke. As I stood talking with him, I noticed he was wearing garbage bags. He had one wrapped around each leg and was wearing one like a coat.

"Aren't you cold?" I asked.

"Nope, but I bet you are," he said.

He was right, I was freezing. He told me how the body generates its own heat and how wearing plastic keeps all your natural body heat from escaping. I gave him a few dollars for the education and went to do my comedy show. Afterwards, he was sitting on one of those grates with the steam coming from below the street.

"This is where I'll sleep tonight," he said.

"How did you become homeless?" I asked.

He told me that he went to Georgetown and was in his last semester of school when he decided to drop out. The pressure of becoming something he never wanted to be was overwhelming to him. He came from a family of lawyers, but was never able to pursue his own dream. Instead, he destroyed theirs and found peace on the streets. I probably could've talked to him all night, but it was cold and the wind was blowing through my coat.

If only he had an extra garbage bag.

Keep Receipts

My grandfather seldom had long conversations with me. He was infamous for giving you a dollar and telling you not to tell anybody where you got it from. His favorite saying was, "I wanna thank ya!" He lived his life to the fullest.

One day I saw him leaving the rental office in his apartment complex. He was angry. It was rare to see him that way. My mother asked him what was wrong and he said that the manager told him he missed paying his rent several months ago. My grandfather told the man he would be back with his receipt to prove he paid his rent and he never missed a payment. He turned to me and said, "Count your own money and always keep a receipt."

I've done that my entire life.

When my son was 18 years old, he came to visit me but arrived with an attitude. I asked him what his problem was and he told me his anger came from me not paying child support. I told him to never accuse a person of anything until you have all the facts. I'm not sure where that thought came from but what he didn't know is that I had every child support payment receipt I ever made. I went down to the file cabinet where I've kept my receipts for years. I took out his file and I placed every cleared child support check on the floor. I put them in order by months and years. I had about 15 rows of checks. I called him downstairs and asked him to tell me what he saw. He looked at the receipts for a moment and said, "I guess I was wrong, you have paid."

"What else do you see?" I asked.

"I don't know what else to say, but I see you paid," he said.

"Stand here until you figure it out," I responded.

After three hours, I explained it all to him.

"I paid every month, but I was late many times. I was self-employed and I sometimes went months without a gig. Yet, every time I worked, I always made up for the month I missed. If you look at the checks you'll notice the different amounts. I sent checks from other people's accounts as I traveled the world to provide for you. Yes, I wish I could have been there throughout your life, but I never forgot you were my son. I sent money orders and money grams. At the end of the day, I paid and I kept every receipt like my grandfather told me."

Afterward, I looked him in the eye and said, "Count your own money and keep your receipts."

One day outside of Houston, Texas in 1990 I got a speeding ticket. I don't procrastinate on settling tickets so as soon as I get one, I pay it immediately. Since I didn't live there, I knew I wasn't going to go to court to fight it. After the ticket was entered into the system, I sent a money order to pay it. I put the receipt in my file cabinet. This should be the end of the story. About eight years later, that particular police department converted to a new computer system to track tickets and violations. Instead of consolidating their records and entering paid tickets into the system prior to the conversion they sent out arrest warrants to everyone who received a ticket between 1990 and 1998. When I read the letter it stated I had 30 days to pay the citation or a warrant for my arrest would be issued. I went to my file cabinet and made a copy of the money order receipt. I also tracked down the money order that was sent and when it was cashed. Case closed. I still have the receipt to this day. James Wilson, my grandfather, was right again.

Meet the Family

When you take a person out on a date and you feel like they could be *the one*, your next date should be the family reunion. You really need to know who raised the person you might want to spend your life with. I've met some great people, then met the family and wondered how they escaped such dysfunction. You need to know who they depend on for support. Dysfunctional issues are in every family, but some issues are on another level. I really try to understand the personalities of the people I deal with so I can stay out of harm's way. At the end of the day, can't we all just get along? We sure can— with the help of medication....

How You Finish

It's not how you start, it's how you finish. The race is not given to the swift or strong, but to those who endure to the end. In 1984, I joined the Army. When I got to my training school, I was in a unit with two guys from Baltimore. We clicked right away and are still friends to this day.

To learn our technical jobs for the Army, we were given 16 weeks to finish school; thereafter we would receive assignments for our permanent duty stations. I finished second in the class and finished about six weeks early. My other two friends failed the course and had to be reclassified into another job. When you failed at the job you chose, you could go home or be reassigned. I finished, but they both failed. Fast forward, all three of us ended up at Fort Hood, Texas several months later. I was a communications (commo) guy and they were in field artillery units. They became tankers.

I earned several awards while stationed at Fort Hood in my field. I was one of the best at my job and was always sent out to deal with the difficult communication problems. Based on my performance and test scores, I was destined to do well in the Army.

After our three-year enlistment was up, one got out and went back to Baltimore. He got a job, had kids and still enjoys coming home after eight hours of work. My other friend who failed his first technical course learned another job skill and reenlisted. He worked and climbed the ladder.

I got out after I did three years of active duty and two years in the National Guard. I ended my career busted down to a private first class with six years of service. On my DD Form 214 (Certificate of Release or Discharge) I earned more awards than making rank. My friend who stayed in after he failed, well, he climbed the military ladder. He ended his career with 24 years of service and the rank of First Sergeant. He's retired, receives a check for the rest of his life, enjoys waking up and letting the day take him wherever. We started out together as young, determined men on a journey to figure out manhood. We encountered some trials and hardships but we maneuvered through the obstacles. Looking back at our Army days I may have finished the class first, but the one who failed conquered the mountain. We still laugh about those days in 31V10 communication school when we get together. We all got up, accepted the challenge and have done well. It's not how you start, but it is how you finish after the fall.

Love

L ove is a word that has taken me many years to understand its relevance in my life. I've always questioned how a person who says they love someone also has the capacity do some of the most heinous things to the person or people they say they love. For me, love is action. It's not the words that move me, but the action behind the scenes that makes me feel loved. I've watched people say how much they love a person, but their actions seem so far from love. If you truly love a person, why would you tear them down?

I've often heard, if you love a person, let them go. If they return it was meant to be. In my opinion if they return, they realized the grass wasn't greener on the other side of the fence. The grass will always be greener where you live if you cut it, water it, fertilize it and maintain it. Do the work that's necessary for love to flourish and you'll never have to test this theory. Love may cause you to do some strange things, but leaving should never be a part of the equation.

I've been married three times and each woman told me how much she loved me, but in the end, love didn't keep my first and second wife from signing divorce papers. Love couldn't overcome what each individual wanted in the relationship. Love wasn't greater than the desires of each person. Our brand of love seems so selfish, but it should be selfless. In John 3:16, it states how God loved the world so much that He sacrificed His only son to bring redemption, salvation, and eternal life. God loved us so much that He didn't just talk about it—He took action! Jesus died for us to prove His love affair with mankind.

After many years I realize that I equate love with action. I read a book called *The 5 Love Languages* and learned that my love language is *acts of service*. Everybody has a love language. If you tell me you love me, I'm waiting to see it manifested by your actions. I know for a fact I would rather be respected than loved. I used to always say in my show as a joke, I'd rather be liked than loved. You see, most women that loved me no longer talk to me, but all the ones that liked me, still do.

What's the point? Understand love for yourself. Love is not just a four letter word. It can be complicated, simple, wonderful and the end of the day, what you make it to be.

Time

My brother preached a sermon many years ago that I think about often. There was a major plane crash and everyone on board was killed, including several people on the ground. He talked about how the passengers on board had no idea that they were about to die. Can you imagine? The plane pushed back from the gate, took off, and in two minutes and forty-seven seconds everyone on board was dead.

My brother posed a question to the congregation and asked, "If you knew you only had less than three minutes to live, what would you do differently?"

I think about that a lot.

He encouraged people to live each day as though they only had a few minutes left. Make good use of your time. After hearing that sermon, I started praying with my children every morning before they went to school. I hugged them just a little tighter than before and told them I'd see them when they got home. If for some reason they didn't make back home, I was thankful that my last time with them was spent in prayer.

Nobody knows what tomorrow will bring, but we all have this moment right now. Each time I sit down to have dinner with my wife, it's Thanksgiving to me. I try to really live in the moment and appreciate what God has given me in spite of my shortcomings. Some close friends lost their mother recently and I'm thankful I got a chance to see her in the hospital before she passed. I didn't tell her goodbye. As I left, I said, "I'll see you later."

Give me my roses now, while I can smell them and know what they are. My mother has dementia of the Alzheimer's type. When I look back over our life together, I'm thankful for each trip I took her on. She may not remember those trips, but even in the cloud of the disease I believe she knows she is loved.

I'm also grateful for the memories I shared with my father. It's been well over a decade since he passed away, but I still laugh out loud when I think of all his antics. In a nutshell, LIVE and live some more. Do it now and don't put it off. Don't just think about doing something; put some action behind those thoughts!

Don't wait, tomorrow is not promised.

Lay in the grass, share a meal, take a drive, visit a friend, help a stranger, do something in your church, speak, smile, hug, laugh, cry, yell, get up, dance, sing, vacation, love, enjoy a movie, walk in the rain, call your ex—OK, that's going too far, but whatever you do, do it *today*.

Don't wait to do the things you think about. Do them before your last two minutes and forty-seven seconds are up.

Laugh!

You should go to a comedy club every month to catch a live show or just go out to see great entertainment. It's a special gift to be able to make people laugh—to stand on stage with a microphone and deliver line after line. When people see my show and tell me I'm the funniest comedian they've ever seen, I say thank you and then ask them how often they go out to see live comedy. They either say I'm the first or they rarely go out to see comedy shows.

Check out your local comedy club. You'll be pleasantly surprised at the level of talent available these days. I love to hear I'm funny, but never the funniest because it's pressure and I know others who are funnier.

The greatest compliment I ever received after a show was from a man who came up to me and said "I've been in therapy for 30 years and your show was the first time in all those years I forgot about my problems. You've done in 30 minutes what my doctors haven't been able to do in years. Thank you for your humor."

Enjoy the arts in your city.

Raising Children

"**M**y kids don't want for nothing." I've heard people make that statement and carry it like a badge of honor. If that's how you want to raise your children, then march to that drum beat. I wanted my kids to have a good life, but I also wanted them to have the experience of working hard to obtain things they wanted.

In life you can't have it *all*, but if you're willing to work, you can certainly enjoy the fruits of your labor. As my children grew, I wanted them to experience disappointment so that I could teach them how to respond and recover. Rejection is real and you'll have to learn how to handle it to overcome adversity. I certainly know what it feels like to be rejected and like the great poet Maya Angelou, I will rise every time I'm knocked down.

Every child shouldn't get a trophy. If you win, here's your prize. If you lose, try again. There's only one Super Bowl ring given to the winner. Some children may not want for anything, but often that translates into the appreciation of nothing.

I've watched parents bend over backwards to give their child everything and cushion the blow from experiencing disappointment. Our parents raised us to be responsible. We are rearing the next generation of children with a level of entitlement. On Saturday mornings when I was growing up, you didn't think about asking to go anywhere until that house was cleaned from top to bottom. These days, kids don't clean and I hear parents say, "I can't do anything with them."

Not on my watch.

My kids cleaned, ironed, made their own beds and, by age 7, woke up to their own alarm clocks. I refused to raise my kids to be weak or vulnerable.

When I was a kid we had one meal for dinner. You either ate it or you went hungry. My mother never made special meals just because you didn't like what was being served. You ate what was on your plate, period, and we threw away NOTHING. You could not like what was in front of you, but at the end of the day you ate it anyway. I remember my brother sitting at the table what seemed like forever because he wouldn't eat. Today's children throw away food, don't eat it all or simply eat fast food junk. My daughter came to visit me once and I prepared her a meal. She told me she didn't like what I had cooked but I told her to eat it anyway. "You should be thankful you have something to eat. There are other children who are hungry," I told her.

She told me to give them hers.

I wasn't going to fix another meal so she left the plate and played outside. I suppose around 9 p.m. that night, the hunger pangs kicked in and she told me she was hungry. I put that plate in the microwave and she ate every bite and asked for seconds. I never had a problem with her eating again.

My children are survivors and they all fight their way through this life. Along the way they may need help, but I'll never take the responsibility for their choices. I'm here to guide and give advice if needed. Their choices are up to them. You have to teach them to stand now in order for them to stand when you can't stand any longer.

Is Race Important?

Back in 2000, I received my Associate of Arts degree in speech communications. I was taking a class about the effect of international relationships on the economy. A student from Jamaica asked why race was so important in the United States. He told us no matter what color you are, if you're born in Jamaica, you're Jamaican. Not African-Jamaican, European-Jamaican or Asian-Jamaican. Just Jamaican.

I totally understood that view, but America is a very complex place—especially when it comes to race.

My father had a plethora of friends from all walks of life. He taught me to respect people and not judge their differences. As I matured, I explored all walks of life and found my groove within various circles. I hung out with nerds, convicts, athletes, homosexuals, drug dealers, Christians and a few rednecks. I've never cared about color, I just wanted to have fun with whomever was having fun.

In my twenties I was exposed to different people from around the country. I learned how to appreciate a person for what they brought to the table. I liked being around people even if they were fake, shallow, introverted, extroverted, or boring as Hell. It was never about their skin color. It was about the way they dealt with me. I looked at their actions and then added up the cost on whether I should stay with the group or move on.

Sometimes you have to know when to fold them.

I went to a party once in Scottsdale, Arizona and the waiter was asking people if they wanted coffee, and if so, how many cubes of sugar. Most people said one or two. When he got to me I said five. The entire party stopped and looked at me. I stirred my five cubes and asked for three more. What did I learn from all the stares? I learned that I need 8 cubes of sugar to enjoy my coffee. What they thought of this, I'll never know.

Once you put race out of your mind you'll see that we are all the same. When I travel internationally and they ask me for my citizenship, I proudly say American.

I've been to Russia, Denmark, Rome, New York, Miami, Cleveland, Aruba, Alabama and many places in between and I've come to one conclusion, no matter the color of the woman, cleavage is cleavage. Men always get excited and look when they see nice cleavage. You'll never hear a man discriminate between Indian-American cleavage, Asian-American cleavage, and Cincinnati cleavage. Let's end all titles and just enjoy being an American in this great country we call home…America is a great country because of all the people that make it unique.

No Place Like Home

There's no place like home. No matter where you go in the world, there's something special about coming home. Home should be comfortable—a place where you can unwind, relax and shut out the troubles of the day. My home has been my safe haven. It's where I go to recharge. There are days that I stand in my backyard and think about the boy that left home at 18 years old with $38 in his pocket, wearing a coat his grandmother bought him. When I look back over my life, I can say that God has been good to me.

When I'm standing in my yard, I often reflect on where I am today and the hurdles I had to jump over to stand in my accomplishments. The reason I love coming home is because of my wife. She has transformed my house into a home. The Bible tells us that 'when a man finds a wife, he finds a good thing.' I have a good thing and I'm thankful for her presence that makes my house a home.

A Chair

I think every man should have a La-Z-Boy chair in his house. Ladies, take notes. He should have a chair no one else sits in. A chair that, when you look at it, you know it's the man of the house's chair. Growing up my dad had a chair and I often stopped guests from sitting in it.

A lady that lived on my street when I was a child gets all the credit for this line of thinking. I remember her husband always sat in the same chair. Whenever I came to the house, he was in his chair and I never saw anyone else sitting in it. One day she bought him a new one and paid over $400 for it. That was a lot of money in the 1970s. I was shocked at the price for a chair. I asked her why she would spend that much money on that chair. She said her husband was a good man. He loved her, and enjoyed being home with the family. A good man deserves a good chair. He worked hard and enjoyed watching TV. He deserved to be treated with respect and honor. More than the chair, I always admired her reverence for him. The chair was a symbol of respect for his headship in the home.

I have a chair, my son-in-law just got his chair and my friend is waiting on his. When will you get yours?

Saving Money

Back in 1997 I saw a news report about people saving money. The reporter stated that the average person spent about $800 a year in coins and if they saved all their change, they could have a nice emergency savings account. After that, I decided to save all of my change. I used it to fund my retirement. Almost 20 years of saving change has added up. When I go to the bank, my wife is embarrassed as I deposit my $3.55 into my retirement account.

There's a new teller working the counter at my bank. I took time to explain to her the method to my madness. She laughed, then thought about it and said she might try the same thing. Even my oldest son laughed about saving change until he tried it. He saved his change for about six months. He made the mistake of counting it and was shocked at the amount. Instead of taking his to the bank, he took a trip to NYC.

A lot of people today, swipe their debit or credit card for purchases. I still use cash about 90 percent of the time when I'm out, so change adds up pretty quickly for me. The main point is to get into a habit of saving. I don't care if it's pennies. We spend our money on the things we want and don't think twice about it, but when it comes to saving a few dollars, we don't make it a priority. As you invest in others, take the time to invest in yourself. Saving change is a good place to start saving money. Build your emergency savings account with your extra change. If you don't have $500 in a savings account while you're reading my book, you need to stop laughing and start counting pennies. Surprisingly they'll turn into dollars. It is better to prepare than not be prepared. Save something...

Your Circle

Best friend, friend, associate, and acquaintance are terms that describe people's relationships with one another. Each term comes with different rules and expectations. You'll never be disappointed with the relationship if you don't cloud the lines between each term. In other words, you can't expect an acquaintance to fulfill the role of a best friend. Nor can you expect a friend to perform on the level of a best friend. Each term carries different levels of trust and responsibilities. You must understand what each term brings to the table.

I have people that wear each of these titles in my life. I'm never upset because I understand their value in my life. My best friend has been there for me in the good and the bad. We have laughed together, cried, argued, fought, encouraged and been there to pick one another up. If you have one best friend you might have more than most. I know for a fact I have several best friends. What makes them a best friend? They listen and will tell me the truth no matter what. They will argue their point and allow me to argue mine. We can agree to disagree and still go have dinner like nothing ever happened. Our feelings are not hurt because we know that we love each other and would do anything for the good of the relationship.

I also have friends. Friends are people I enjoy being around and love socializing with. We talk often and plan to get together for any occasion to enjoy the moment. Associates are people I may come in contact with from time to time. It's great to see them when I see them, but if I don't, that's OK too. I might not see them for years but when I do, we'll pick up right where we left off. Yet, I'm not necessarily inviting an associate that lives out of town to my family gatherings like I would a friend. And I'm not likely going to their kid's graduation or attending their church Christmas play. I'll give them a ride if they need one, but if I can't I'm not losing any sleep. In contrast, for a best friend I'll get up in the middle of the night and give a ride to wherever they needed to go. For an associate, if I hear something has happened in their life, I may offer a hand or say a prayer on their behalf. That's not mean, it's just the truth. Acquaintances are last on the list. I can take them or leave them. These are people I know in passing. We may work together on occasions or know some of the same people. A guy I knew for years told me to keep his name out of my mouth. No problem, never said it again.

To determine the relationship, I look at the value a person brings to my life. I consider what I would miss if we no longer communicated. If my best friend is hurt, I am hurt. If they're in need, so am I. That's how we roll. You just can't offer that same level of commitment to everyone you know or meet. It's not realistic.

I've met many people in my life and there's not one city I can travel to and not find a person that fits into one of the terms above, but there are few places where I can lay my head and be comfortable. Every city is a homecoming for me. My relationships stretch from the east to the west, north to the south and all points in between. I truly respect all the relationships I've discussed. If I didn't, I wouldn't revel in bliss when I cross paths with my best friends, friends, associates, and acquaintances. Understand the importance of the people in your life and enjoy the ride!

Matthew 7:7-8

Read Matthew 7:7-8. These two scriptures will change your life if you understand the power behind them. The power to change is in you. If you would heed the words of these scriptures your tomorrow will be better than your yesterday.

The first thing you need to do is *ask*. What is it that you need, want or desire? Ask for it by name. After you ask, you must seek what you asked for. Seeking demonstrates a desire to obtain or achieve. The last step is to knock and wait for the door to be opened. All three phases of these two scriptures require movement on your part and your reward is on the other side of the door opening. Problem is—most people are lazy.

God sees your need and if you do your part, He'll do His. Stop living a defeated life when the power is in your movement of faith. Faith without works is dead. Many people ask, but never move forward. They sit and complain while waiting on the Lord. They ask for a job, but never go out seeking and knocking for the door to open. Each day we have the opportunity to be a witness to the goodness of God. Believe that your life will change, and it will. You don't have to read *The Secret* to know that the secret is in the scriptures.

What's truly a secret is that many people don't read. I never wanted to be an 'assembly required' type of father.

My dad was one, and I chose to break the mold. What is an assembly required father? I'll tell you. Every Christmas I'd receive a gift that needed to be assembled. My dad would never read the instructions on how to put the toy together. Instead, he would look at the picture on the box and proceed to putting it together. There were always extra pieces left over that were never used. Hence, the toy never worked like it did on TV. I would think to myself, if only he would read the instructions I would be playing with my toy right now. The Bible has the master set of instructions on how to live. Stop looking at society for your instructions on how to live victoriously. Just read.

Hyphenated Names

I've noticed over the last several years that more women are hyphenating their last names. I'm not sure what it means until I ask the person. It could be to honor someone that played an important role in their life. What I do know is that when it comes to marriage, if your wife hyphenates her name and keeps another name before yours, your marriage is divided.

Once you marry a man, you take his name and become one with him. Your daddy, grandfather or your strong, independent mother's name does not take precedence over the man you become one with. If he's not able to succeed as head of your life, then not only should you not take his name you shouldn't marry him either. It seems that whoever's name is before the husband's last name will take precedence in decision making. The name before the hyphen will be honored first.

You can't be one with two last names.

Today there is a concentrated effort to remove the man as the head of the household. *Good Times* was a great show until they removed 'James' from the cast. It never had the same feeling and the harmonious balance was lost. The family is dying because men are not standing up and taking the responsibility to lead their family. If you can't take his last name then stay with your parents, by yourself, grandfather or whoever raised you until a man worthy enough finds you. When he does, take his name with pride. There is nothing wrong with honoring others who have played an important part of your life, but when the two become one, they should have one last name.

Greatness and Heroism

Great and hero. As a youth, I don't ever remember hearing these words to describe someone as much as they do today. First, I had to research the definitions of both words. *Great* is defined as intensity, considerably above the normal or average. A *hero* is a man of distinguished courage or ability, admired for his brave deeds and noble qualities. A woman can be a hero since the word is gender neutral or she can be called a heroine.

Now that I have established the foundation for both words, I'd like to delve into my confusion with the overuse of these words today.

Everything can't be great nor should everyone be labeled a hero. Some things are good. In the Bible, God created the world and He said it was good. I can live with good—especially when God says so.

Harriet Tubman was a hero based on her actions to free slaves. She risked her life for the good of others. Nelson Mandela was a hero for his contribution to end apartheid in South Africa. He was imprisoned for decades and went on to become the president of the country he loved after his release. Now these are great testaments to define a hero.

People like Harriet Tubman and Nelson Mandela are in a class of their own, but these days everybody is great— great teacher, great pastor, great coach, great nurse, great, great, great, and greater. What are we comparing the word to? I'm not sure how to measure greatness when I look at all that God did in creating the world and He called it *good*. Either way, I feel the term is overused today in every walk of life. I think Richard Pryor was a great comedian. He changed the game and was able to infiltrate all genres from stand up to television, stage and films. I believe one of the greatest players to ever play in the NBA was Allen Iverson. At six-feet-tall and 165 pounds, he could take over the game. He could play the entire game, hated to come out and played with intense passion. You can't teach that type of passion, either you have it or you don't. Some may disagree because I used the word *great*. They'll find other athletes and call them great. My point is that we just overuse the word today. Great and hero are words that should truly be reserved for great achievements.

Success

My mother used to walk home from the bus stop with the other mothers in the neighborhood every evening after work. The only thing she ever required was that her house was clean and the air conditioner was on when she came home. She loved to feel the cool air when she entered the house after walking a mile in the heat.

During their walk, the mothers would often talk about their children. At times, my mother would share some of the stories from those conversations with me. Sadly, some of the comments were 'my son just got out of jail' or 'he's still dealing with his drug problem.' I never wanted mom's hard work to be in vain. I always wanted her to be able to speak well of me to her friends.

If your parents worked hard to give you a solid platform to jump off into life, the least you can do is repay them by being productive. Some people measure success by fame and fortune. I've measured success by doing whatever it takes to enjoy life. I've worked with some of the most successful people in the world, but my true joy in life was being a husband and a father.

Many nights when I lived in Los Angeles I could've gone out with famous entertainers, but I always chose to go home. Home was where I wanted my success to come from. Now I sit back and watch my daughter raise her kids.

I laugh because she sounds like a parent and I see the hard work of parenting has paid off. My kids are successful and live on their terms. I step in from time to time to guide and give them my old-fashioned forty-five minute lecture, but in the end they make decisions that best serve them.

I'm thankful I had the opportunity to take my mom on vacations to Hawaii, the Bahamas, Alaska and numerous other trips. Find something or someone in your life that you don't want to let down and let that thought propel you into your destiny.

God is Awake. Go to Sleep!

My father was full of humorous and wise one-liners. Only he wasn't trying to be funny. He just spoke his mind and didn't care where it landed. One afternoon he was on the phone dealing with a bill collector. He was telling the representative how they could handle the situation amicably. They went back and forth. I heard my dad say at the end, "Alright, I'll handle it after I hang up!!" He hung up the phone and got in the bed.

"I thought you were going to handle it," I said.

"I am," he confidently replied.

"But, you're in bed," I said with doubt.

"That's how I'm going to handle it—by getting some sleep. God is on the throne. Ain't no sense in both of us being up!"

Point taken.

Read

I know for a fact that the Bible is the greatest book ever written. I'm not an avid reader. I'm a research reader. When I need to uncover some truth, or prepare for a speaking engagement, I read diligently. I love to read autobiographies. I enjoy reading the story behind the success or failure of a person. Every once in a while I'll get a book that challenges my perspective or enhances my thought process. In my twenties I read three books that I feel every young man should read to prepare him for the journey ahead: *Way of the Peaceful Warrior*, *Point Man*, and *Who Moved My Cheese?*

Each book allowed me to understand my position in life and helped me realize my worth as a man. I learned to create multiple streams of income from *Who Moved My Cheese?* Being self-employed, you must understand the highs and lows of your business. I was able to learn the trends and stay ahead of failure by preparing myself to always be in position to succeed. I was always in pursuit of creating something else that I could use to provide for my family. I didn't want to have an excuse for not being able to provide. I stayed vigilant in moving forward and gathering all my resources to meet the demand of the needs of those I loved. Each time I walked through the door of my home, I wanted my wife and kids to know that I had their best interest in mind and I never wanted them to suffer due to my poor choices.

Way of the Peaceful Warrior is a journey. We are all on a journey looking for the pinnacle of success, meaning of life, or our definition of happiness. This book deals with seeking guidance as you pursue life's challenges. It talks about the importance of a mentor and how he or she can help you avoid pitfalls.

A friend of mine gave me *Point Man*. I read a few chapters and was confused about why I was given the book. Everything it talked about, I lived. I was that man who loved his wife, children and embraced everything about providing for my house. I didn't have any of the issues the book discussed. I started to return the book when I realized that all men didn't get *it*. Men go through different things and this book helped me to see some of the struggles of men from different angles. As I continued to read, I was also able to focus on shortcomings I didn't believe I had when I first began reading the book. It became a good read and I learned how to communicate with other men on a deeper level.

I still apply the principles of these books in my life even some 20 years later. My son now has two young sons. I'm sure in his quest to be a better father he'll find material that will shed light on the road he'll prepare for them. I paved the way for him to the best of my ability and walked upright in truth.

I know he'll do the same.

Ripping and Running

If I don't know anything else about my generation, I know this: WE NEVER STAYED IN THE HOUSE. We played outside *every* day. Our parents had to make us come into the house. There were only a few fat kids when I grew up and you could count them on one hand. Unfortunately, these days there are more overweight children in our neighborhoods than ever.

I thank God for being able to rip and run when I was a child. I'm saddened by the plight of children these days. I enjoyed and relished my childhood. I knew most of the families on my street and wasn't afraid to go anywhere in my community. When I was a kid, we had parents and people in the community who cared and worked hard to help you become somebody. Every house had two parents and you called them Mr. and Mrs. So-and-So, but never by their first names.

We didn't have a watch to tell time, but we watched the movement of the street to know what was going on. When the school bus came in the afternoon, you knew it was around 3:30 p.m. When you had to go in to eat, it was around 6 p.m. When the ice cream man came, it was around 7 p.m. When the street lights came on you were around your house and it was almost time to go in. Time was never exact. We just sort of knew when to move. Every kid on our street came outside and played, allowing us to get to know each other.

I live on a street now with over 30 houses on it and I hardly ever see children at play. I know my neighbors to the left and right, but other than that, my street is full of strangers. I don't know their kids and they don't know me. We're strangers in our own expensive communities. I can't call it my neighborhood because I don't know anything about the families on my street. Even to this day when I go back home to Baltimore, I can walk down my old street and remember who lived where. I remember their names and stories about each house. I remember who had the best house parties, where parents trusted us enough to entertain ourselves in the basement, grooving to house music and slow jams. You hoped the parents allowed you to turn off all the lights so you could get a slow dance and feel on some girl's booty. I often wake up in a cold sweat over this generation. I never questioned whether I would live to see 18. These children do not have that same peace.

I also remember when my grandmother would have me go ask Mrs. Betty for a cup of sugar or two eggs. Whatever my grandmother made, she would have me take something to Mrs. Betty after she finished. We borrowed and nobody talked about it or looked down on you for asking. Today, we're afraid to ask for assistance in fear of being talked about. With the fluctuating price of gas these days you better put pride aside and ask for help when the road gets tough.

We must get back to the LOVE we had for our neighborhoods and look out for the children. There's diminished respect and discipline today, therefore, our children are suffering. Let's get back to parenting so our children can enjoy ripping and running as we did.

Search for Purpose

I enjoyed watching the film, *Into the Wild*. It was about a young man looking for answers. He pondered whether he should travel down the path that was already paved or figure out the true meaning of life for himself. I thought the movie had a meaningful storyline. I loved the fact that it was real and I could see myself taking a similar journey to find certain answers that I've pondered my entire life. That's probably why I walk a great deal, to think and figure out what to do next as I close in on retirement.

I've often thought about reinventing myself. After three decades of standup comedy, would could I do? I thought about being a truck driver. Several people wanted me to start a church. Maybe I could open an ice cream store and create all the flavors I love. When I was 21 years old, I set lifetime goals that I wanted to achieve and I reached all of them before I turned 40. Now I'm trying to figure out what to do next as I receive my monthly AARP newsletters.

I'd like to help kids, but they have guns these days. Maybe I could help parents, but they have guns, too. There's entirely too much shooting going on. I'm a comic, not a warrior. I tried to be a mentor, but I was told I was terrible at mentoring. Apparently I set the bar too high for men to jump over. 'Get up and take care of your family,' I say. Now why is that too high? I encourage you to watch the movie. I asked my son to watch it and he fell asleep before the opening credits. He said it wasn't fast enough for him. He'll probably appreciate it now that he has children. Now he gets to walk in my shoes. I can't wait for his sons to show him their report cards. The one thing I know about life is this: if you live long enough you'll walk down many paths. You'll see some of the same things your forefathers saw, but you'll handle it differently. At least you think you will. I just get to sit back, observe and take notes....

Stop Picking

The Bible clearly states *what God brings together*, not who you pick or who you think you want to be with, but who He joins together, *let no one separate*. Instead of praying for a mate, we pick who we think is the right person for us and then we pray for God to fix the other person to suit us.

When you are in your dating phase you need to look for the qualities of a man that are equal to or greater than what you know. Many women are raised without their father and really don't know what to look for in a man. They tend to choose a mate based on looks, status or what they think they want. If they were raised by a good man it becomes even harder to find a man that will have the qualities she found in her father.

Today's households are led mainly by single women therefore, the young girls don't know what they need and the young boys can't give them what they deserve. The boys are accustomed to a woman maintaining the household, fixing, providing and solving the issues that the family deals with. Today's young man has no problem with his wife, girlfriend or baby mama doing the same as what their own mother did. These men tend to put their mothers first since she never left them while doing her best to provide a safe place for them. Many children are leaving home not prepared to take care of a home.

We are lacking basic understanding of the roles each person has in a relationship. I'm just saying, a man needs to lead and a woman needs to support the leadership. Problem is most women can't trust the man because she has been failed before by the man living in *her* house. I've told my daughters, if a man can't elevate you then leave him where he is until he's worthy to be responsible for your life. It's his job to provide. Understand your role is to submit. I know it's hard to submit if your man keeps losing his job, needs his mama to loan him money and is driving your car. That's why you wait for the Lord to prepare the person that will benefit your life. Stop picking and start praying.

Iron Sharpens Iron

The best line I ever heard at a wedding from a father to his new son-in-law: "Your feet are always welcome to rest under my table." That line almost made me cry. Not tears of sadness. I get emotional when I see men embracing and showing younger men what it takes to be a real man. In essence he was telling his new son-in-law to stop by at any time he would felt the weight of life on his shoulders or was world-weary. The father was opening his door to future conversations and offering himself as a guide to navigate his new role as husband.

There is no greater honor than to break bread in the home of a man you respect. He created a safe harbor for him to rest his feet. When I see a father and son showing love to one another, I applaud. Mothers have always been there, but many fathers have been absent. It's getting rare to see an athlete give credit to his father for standing watch over his development. I know some good men who are putting in the time to enhance the lives of their sons. Proverbs 27:17 tells us that "Iron sharpeneth iron; so a man sharpeneth the countenance of his friend." When men stand up, we can save the family, church, community, and even the country.

Childhood

I've never lost that kid feeling on the inside. I still love watching *The Flintstones*. My grandmother used to watch a soap opera called *The Edge of Night* and as soon as it went off, I'd lose my mind watching my favorite cartoon.

My heart still skips a beat when I hear the bells of the ice cream truck. Eddie Murphy did the best ice cream joke ever in *Delirious*. We would run to wherever the truck stopped. Kids would get their money and be in line within 20 seconds.

The smell of fresh cut grass on a hot day reminds me of two-a-days in August. My football folks now what I'm talking about. I'm thankful to still have my senses. I've enjoyed each phase of my life.

I remember when I left home to attend college in August of 1983. I sat in front of the dorm until 4:00 am. I just wanted to stay out all night because I could. My dad told me I didn't know how good I had it and that I'd want to return home under his roof in no time. Not me.

Not once in my life have I ever wanted to return to living under my father's authority. I love being an adult and on my own. I love drinking a milkshake and making that noise with the straw because nothing else is in the cup. My mother used to tell me to stop, but I wanted to get every drop.

Trouble is still my favorite board game. It's the only board game we played as a family. Even my dad enjoyed that game. I played it with my kids. I think everyone should take some time to write about their life and see how the pieces connect that make you, YOU. I'm not sure who came up with the statement or phrase that once we are born, we are living the dash until our death. I'm thankful for my dash and all it has encompassed.

My childhood was the foundation for my adult years. I took the hand that was given me and I'm playing it to the max. Things that I saw as a child that I didn't like, I've tried to correct those ways for the future of my own kids. I refused to bring a generational curse along for the ride. I tried to develop my own philosophies and make the world a better place.

Stop blaming someone or something that keeps you from greatness. At this moment, you can change your tomorrow by forgiving and moving on with the rest of your dash. Only you can keep yourself in bondage. Childhood is a start but adulthood is the goal. Enjoy life!!!

Full Circle

This is what it's all about. I feel like my purpose in life is to help my children walk into their own destiny, be an example to the young men I meet and represent the God I know. I'm not sure how fathers can turn their back on their children and look themselves in the mirror every morning. For my 50th birthday, I didn't want a party. I just wanted to have dinner with my children. As I sat in the restaurant looking at my kids on my 50th birthday, I was overcome with emotion. I was moved and encouraged when I was talking to my youngest son and realized that he is a man now. He understood the lessons I taught him. It was a small gesture but a big gesture for me to witness. He allowed his girlfriend to go first as he handed her a plate. It was the respect he had for her that told me, he's going to be OK and she's in good hands. It was more than just a dinner with my kids—it was resting in the fact that they are all right. I gave them all of me and in return I now get to have peace about their own futures.

It's a satisfying feeling when your kids make you proud. It's good to cherish the moments. If I could go back in time, I would go back to the time I use to fly them into bed, hug them and call them my little birdies.

All I can say is everything we've endured was worth the struggle. I am so grateful that my wife worked with all of my children to make sure they were all at the table with me on such a special day in my life. It was truly a full circle moment. Great way to turn 50!!!

AARP Card

I must say, 50 feels great! Even though I am 50, I feel much younger. Don't worry—I won't be wearing black socks with sandals anytime soon. I can still jog, play basketball, golf, and even hit the tennis ball a couple of days a week. I still want to lose some weight. I have been doing well, but ice cream tends to take over my mind, body and soul.

I have noticed that getting out of bed requires additional time and stretching until my body starts to warms up. I need reading glasses and find myself looking for them just like my mother. I still do my own lawn, but if I can find someone that will do it like me, I'll give that up in a heartbeat.

I've planned for retirement and I'm looking forward to doing so when I turn 60. Now that I have my RV, I'm anxious to travel at my own leisure. I want a nice camera to take pictures of places I want to see. I've been everywhere, but I've seen nothing. Often I am so busy working that I do not take time to really see where I am. I want to go back to the places I've worked and truly see and experience the town and the locals. I want to take my time and enjoy the scenery, take long lunches and even longer dinners.

I plan to make a few changes during the second half of my life. What changes? You'll have to wait until I turn 75.

Right now I'm embracing my AARP card and watching my grandkids grow.

Divorce

Divorce is like a cancer that never gets treated. It affects more than the two people who are divorcing. It can tear up families and friendships. Innately, people tend to choose a side to stay on. I've gone through divorces and ever since my kids were young I always disclosed my failures with them. I talked about them having all their children with the same person; my prayer is for that person to be their husband or wife.

Raising a blended family was challenging and problematic at times. It's tough enough raising a family born under the union of marriage. Can you imagine when you add in additional fathers, mothers, grandparents and different DNA? You really have to keep a level head and never take it personal when you hear views that conflict and differ with yours. I think the only time God allows divorce is when someone has been unfaithful. I've come to the conclusion many marriages should have never taken place or they happened because of the wrong reasons or intentions.

Most people have heard the scripture that speaks of the power of God's blessing on a marriage. What God has joined together, let no man put asunder. It's about what God puts together, not who we pick, what we want, or feel responsible for. People join in wedlock for all kinds of reasons from financial benefits, unplanned pregnancy, and potential fame. Some even marry because they are actually attracted to their mate.

In the end, the only marriages that last are the ones where both people work daily to enjoy the love they have for one another. Marriages last because of the relationship between the two people who chose to say 'I do.' There's marriage and being married. I think there are more people married rather than in marriages. What is the difference? If your spouse is your best friend and you do a ton of things together and love spending time with one another, you're in a marriage. If you always hear, 'y'all get on my nerves' from your friends or you never see one without the other, that's marriage.

If you didn't even know the person had a spouse, that's being married. If you rarely see them with their significant other but always see him with his boys or her with her girls, they're married. Married people have two different lives but meet up in a common area at the end of the day. This is not rocket science. If you prefer to spend most of your time away from the person you walked down the aisle with, you're probably married.

Other signs of marriage include thinking of each other's needs first. Married people think of themselves first, their wants and what other people want. People in a marriage think of their needs first and then consider what the other wants. When you sync all of these indifferences together, divorce is closer than one would believe. Consequently, these are some of the causes of the high divorce rate in America. It really comes down to what people want. When wants outweigh needs, the marriage fails. I never wanted to just be married; I wanted to be in a marriage where I came first. If the person that you are married to is not first, then your situation is divided. A divided house will always fall.

Mistakes

You can't live 50 years and not acknowledge some of the lessons you've learned from your mistakes. As long as you have another chance to wake up, you have the opportunity to correct your mistakes. I have my share of liability I feel I must rectify and repair. Moving forward I will honor the mothers of my children every year.

I had this rule that I developed in my mind about Mother's Day. Since they weren't my mother, I chose to honor my own mother on that day. I never called to wish them a Happy Mother's Day, never sent a card, flowers or anything to say thank you for bringing my children into this world. They were my exes and I left it at that.

I believed I was justified for that way of thinking; surely no one could tell me otherwise.

It wasn't until I recognized the individual traits and qualities my children embodied that I had remorse for being selfish and egotistical. I realized that I couldn't take all the credit, nor could I take all the blame. Whatever their mothers and I didn't do to finish the journey together, they would always be a part of me. Admittedly, I failed them in that area. I did pay my child support and have my kids during the summers, but I didn't think enough to say "It's your day and thank you for bringing me these souls to provide for," to their mothers. Moving forward I will acknowledge their importance and express my remorse for my blind misstep and poor judgment in saluting them.

I'm the eldest of the four children in our family. I have a brother only a few years younger than me, but we've never been close. I love him, but we live on different ends of the street. I'm out there shaking hands and talking all the time. He's laid back and somewhat of an introvert. However, my youngest brother and I live on the same street and move at the same speed. We enjoy a lot of the same things in life. We both talk trash and keep the laughs flowing. As for the brother right under me, I know his characteristics, but I really don't *know* him. I don't know how he feels about life in general. I don't know about his dreams, regrets, or goals. Sometimes our dissociations may turn into sibling rivalry, a misunderstanding or simply a disagreement.

He's never done anything to me, but I know I've let him down. I watch how he guides his own sons and protects them to a degree that probably seems overbearing, yet I know it's probably because of what he missed from dad and me—having an older brother to turn to and a father to have spent quality time with.

For me, my dad was great. He did his thing and allowed me to do mine. He did the best he could so I took that and tried to do more with my sons. My brother did the same thing. He's been a part of every aspect of their lives. He did it the right way and had all his eggs in the same basket.

We may not always see eye to eye, but I look forward to getting to know both of my brothers before it's too late.

As I've said, time heals all hurts, but regret lives forever. Maybe we'll plan a brothers fishing trip with our sons one day.

Choices

Choice, Change, Work is the lecture title for my public speaking engagements at grade schools. The lecture deals with the choices people make, the changes that must occur for the choice to come to pass, and the work that must be done for their choices to be effective. I know that may sound like a tongue twister, but it's really simple to comprehend.

We make choices every day. That's the easiest thing to do, choose between one and the other. Say you choose to be rich. Great, now that you've made that choice, what comes next? A change must occur for you to obtain the choice of being rich. For example, a dental hygienist may go back to school to become a dentist. That's the change that must occur for that person to be rich.

Finally, you have to put in the work to become rich. Most people drop the ball on the work aspect. If we don't change our habits, we can't complain about the outcome. Students may want better grades, but they must begin to study more and choose not to stay out all night. Many people want more, but very few do the work. The work is the most important aspect of the entire lecture. If you put in the work, success is guaranteed.

Your Word

Your word is your bond. I often think of this and I try to honor the words I speak. In the movie *Scarface*, Tony Montana said, "All I have in this world is my balls and my word and I don't break 'em for no one, you understand?" I truly, truly, truly feel that if it comes out of your mouth you need to honor what you said. Be committed to the things you said you were going to do. People are depending on what they heard you say or what you said you would do. Disappointment is a result from not being a person of your word. I know in your mind your intent sounds good and you probably have every intention to fulfill your promise, but if you lack execution somebody will ultimately be let down. Think before you commit and execute after you speak.

Help, Not Enable

What is it all about? It's about living in the dash. We know the beginning, but we don't know the end. What we do know is that we are all living the dash at this very moment. Make sure your dash counts. My grandmother taught me to help others. She would help anyone at any time and she wanted nothing in return. Over the years I've noticed that many people don't help. Instead, they take the responsibility or they enable the person to the point they never fully can stand on their own.

I stand today because my father made me walk home in the rain. I stand today because I had people depending on me and quitting was not an option. I had help, but I didn't have crutches. We cripple our kids today by not allowing them to fall and get back up on their own. We want to soften the blow. Life is a daily grind, but it's rewarding if you have the tools to persevere. I encourage everyone to make their own choices, but be responsible for the choices you make. Stop making choices and expecting others who had nothing to do with your choice take on your responsibility. On the streets they would tell you to handle your business. Allow your children to raise their own children or you'll never enjoy your senior years. Bottom line, you got through and now you need to allow them the opportunity to do the same.

Legacy

I want to honor the person I've tried to pattern my life after—my maternal grandmother. She had nine children and I have no idea how many grand, great-grand, and great-great-grandchildren there are today, but I do know this, we all were her favorite. She loved unconditionally, she told the truth and wasn't afraid of anyone. She was a deeply religious woman who helped without wanting anything in return. She made sure everybody got something when the ice cream truck came around. If she didn't have enough money for all, then no one got anything.

She may have had her favorites, but to this day I do not know who they were. She treated us all the same. She would sing and I never knew what song or the words she was singing. She would hold spit in her mouth and then spit it in a cup she kept on the stove. I don't know why. She was the center for all her children. Because of her love, when she got old her children took turns caring for her at home. She was never placed into a nursing home; the siblings took turns throughout the day and overnight to provide for their mother. Those same children are now helping my siblings and I care for our mom as she deals with dementia. My grandmother deposited love and affection in all of us and it's still paying dividends to this day. My grandmother, Mary Wilson is still number one.

Baby Boomer vs. Millennial

Trying to raise this next generation can be tough. I wrote this letter as a guideline for parents that have 30-year-old children living in their house. I hope this helps and puts a little perspective on how to deal with this entitled generation.

First and foremost there must be a level of respect in a home for parents and children to live in harmony. That's how God designed it to be. God, who never makes mistakes, set an order in which the family revolves. Order is present in every aspect of our lives. If you follow order then all will be well with the situation. If you go against the order of life, then you must be prepared to deal with the consequences. Ephesians 6:1-4 tells fathers not to provoke their children to wrath and many children use that scripture when they are dealing with their parents. Before a child can use the scripture, they must look at the order in which the scripture flows. It says to obey your parents first. So if the child honors the father and mother first, then there should never be a reason for a father to provoke his children.

God places the headship in the father. The father is the covering for the family. Therefore, in order to have a long life, you must obey the parents. This is the first commandment that comes with a promise.

There are a few points I want to bring out and a few things that need to be understood in my house before you return. First of all it's not your room. It's my room in my house. As a child you are allowed to occupy the room until the time comes for you to leave and be on your own. I pay the bills, so the room belongs to me. You must keep the room up to my standard. If you're paying rent to live in that room then you can keep it any way you like (rent for the room and bathroom is $300.00 a month). That's how the world works. If you're paying for it then you can do with it what you want. If you're not the one paying then you have to follow the rules whether you like it or not. When there's authority it's good if you understand, but if you don't understand then I recommend for you to do as you're told. On a job there's a procedure you must follow in order to keep your job. You can't change the procedure because you don't feel like it or you feel it's my job and I can do it the way I like.

Here's a list of rules and regulations that must be followed upon your return home.

1. Respect will always come first for your mother.
2. Your speaking volume and tone will never exceed any adult who is correcting you in my house.
3. Your room, including your closet and bathroom, will be clean and kept in an orderly fashion.
4. You will clean the kitchen nightly. This includes putting up the food, cleaning all counters, stove, and microwave, and sweeping if necessary.
5. You can have company as long as we know who they are and they are in the family room.

6. Curfew is 11 p.m., Sunday through Friday and 12 a.m. on Saturday. Permission must be given if time will be later. You must ask first.
7. Church is every Sunday at 10 a.m.

If you have a car, you will discuss your whereabouts with us before you leave. You will not just say I will be back. It's as simple as 'I'm going to the mall,' or 'I'm going to drop off something at school or work and will be back in an hour.' It's to inform us.

Last, I want you to write a letter to your parents about what you learned from this ordeal. How has it affected you? How has it changed you? What do you want from them moving forward? How do you see their roles in your life and decisions? What can improve your relationship with your parents?

If you can agree to the terms and the letters have been written to your parents, then you're welcomed back. If you need to discuss any of this or you're not clear, then we need to talk about it before you return. Don't agree if you have any reservations, concerns or misconceptions of what's expected. If all minds are clear, then sign below.

Approved_____

Things I'm Known for Saying

❝Marriage is simple, if the two people are in a marriage and understand their roles. Not just married, but, in a marriage. Married people have learned how to survive together and marriage is a relationship that continues to grow. What is your role in a marriage? If you don't know, that's why so many end in divorce."

❝How many people really know what they want? Life is based on choices and taking the responsibility for your choice. Conflict occurs when others take the responsibility away from the person that made the choice."

❝When a young girl has a good father; a man will have a great wife."

❝What's it all about? It's about living the dash. We know the beginning, but we don't know the end. What we do know is that we are all living the dash at this very moment. Make sure your dash counts."

"Your feet are always welcome to rest under my table." — The best line I ever heard at a wedding from a Father-in-Law said to his new Son-in-Law.

"I don't know what's going on in the world. I'm just trying to get to Tuesday."

"Take the time to say thank you."

"There's no place like home. No matter where you go in the world, there's something special about coming home."

"I talk to myself, but God answers."

"This is something I know."

"Enjoy the ride!"

Find a Good Church Home

I've been going to church since I was a child. It's a part of who I am. As an adult, I don't go just because it's something to do. I go because I love being a part of a body of believers that enjoy the fellowship. People attend church for many different reasons—tradition, proximity and even the way the building looks may play a role.

Sometimes the church can be filled with drama. I've been to my share of church meetings that made me think I was at a City Hall board meeting trying to pass new legislation.

For the most part, it's a wonderful fellowship and a blessing to be a part of a loving church family. The church has always been an extension of my family. I've grown spiritually from being part of some good churches with pastors that not only could preach, but were also good teachers. Although I've had friends that were hurt by the church, I'm thankful to have never experienced that. When they tell me the church hurt them, I've always asked who hurt them. Most times it's a church leader—even the pastor. The church is a place and I'm not sure how a place can hurt you. Maybe it can, but I feel sometimes people take their focus off God and place it on man. Man can and will fail you, but God never will. When I join a church I'm looking for the message to be a blessing to encourage me or help me to become a stronger person of faith. I go to be recharged, enjoy the music and getting to know people that seek the same thing as I do. I don't go because my family attends. I don't go because my father is the Pastor. I don't go because of the building. I go because it's teaching me how to be better. I want to support and be a part of the vision God has laid out for his people through the pastor. Church is a place that recharges my daily battery. The preached word keeps me refueled and inspired to do better. Joining a church should enhance your life as you learn to get closer to God. Find a place to worship and allow the words that are preached to build your faith and prepare you to lead others to the saving knowledge of God.

Mount Everest

I've finally finished *50 Posts and a Piece of Toast* and realized that I didn't really know as much as I thought. What I'm sincerely trying to say is that I *thought* I knew a great deal about life. In my final analysis, I truthfully knew only a small amount about life. There's so much more to learn, to explore and to be a part of. I've probably just given you a snippet of my life's challenges. You've had your own experiences and your personal journey will differ. Our life events may be parallel or they can be totally, off-the-wall different.

I'm not even sure if this book will make sense or trigger you to write your own story. Either way, my intent was to shed light on some of my thoughts and learning experiences throughout the first 50 years of my life. I've never defined success about the amount of money a person has or can make. I've always looked at success with these few questions: Do you enjoy what you're doing? Are you happy? Are you fulfilled? Are you able to take care of your responsibilities? Success will be however you define it.

In the grand scheme of things, I equated life to climbing Mount Everest. At some point many people may have the chance to reach all of the goals they set for themselves in life. I call this the *Mount Everest Experience*. Allow me to share my mountaintop experience. After my failed marriage, my life was at a standstill. It seemed like I was stalled in first gear. I wasn't moving forward or in reverse. I was just waking up each day with no focus, no drive and no purpose. I was just in a state of existence, not knowing what to do next. Everything that I thought I knew and that I was familiar with no longer existed. Wife was gone, kids were gone, but I was thankful to wake up and still have a chance at living.

When a man loses his purpose, he just sits down. I was confused and my passion was not essential.

I've always enjoyed watching *National Geographic* shows. I enjoy learning about animals' survival, how the earth evolves and going to far off lands. One day I was watching a program about Mount Everest. The announcer was saying that when a person dies on the mountain, their body stays there. There are hundreds of dead bodies buried on the path to the summit. As new climbers are trying to reach the peak, they'll see the other climbers that failed to reach their goal. It must be discouraging to see frozen dreams ended as you continue to pursue yours. Yet, each climber continues their trek despite the obstacles and anxieties with the sole goal of reaching the top.

While I was lost and confused I went back to my childhood home. I stood in the driveway of my parent's home thinking about my life and what was next for me. I stood there watching the cars go up and down the street. People driving to wherever they needed to go. I had no place to go so I stood there and thought for a while. I kept thinking about Mount Everest. I kept thinking about those that made it to the top and the ones that didn't. You prepare your climb and you say your goodbyes, not knowing if you'll reach the top or come back alive. Just like marriage. You get married, but who really thinks about divorce on the wedding night? It's not until you are fully engaged in your marriage that you think about what could happen down the road. It's only after you face some challenges that you begin to explore other options and alternative ways to resolve issues.

I'm sure the climbers on Mount Everest didn't turn around the moment the weather changed. They were prepared for that. They continued on just like you would in your marriage. You make the adjustments, but you keep moving forward and trek up the mountain.

As I stood in the driveway, a clear picture of where I was in my life unfolded in front of me. Here I was 20 years into my career as a comedian, married for 15 years and now lost. When I became a comedian I had simple goals. To buy a car off the showroom floor, make $100,000 a year and buy a house I could live in forever. As I stood there, I realized I had achieved every one of my goals. I had climbed my Mount Everest and fulfilled the goals that I had set for my career and put my life into motion. I had reached the summit. I had prepared, took all the blows, and now that I was at the top of everything I had ever worked for, what's the result of it all? The view was beautiful, but at that point in my life I looked back to see the bodies that were left on the trail. Like I said earlier, when you die on your quest to reach the summit, your body is frozen in time. The bodies on Mount Everest have not changed. Each person that ascends to the top will pass those that didn't make it. My drive was to reach my goals and provide a life for my family. I did that.

Here's where life changes or at least, changed for me. Once you reach the top and you've enjoyed the views, you come down and then you share how to get to the top with others that are willing to listen. Life is all about planning, preparing and achieving in order to carve out a slice of life for you. That's all I ever wanted to do—teach and prepare my children for their life's journey. To protect my family and help those I could along the way. I've always believed in sharing the pie. I did all that I set out to do. I got to the top. And while I thought I was confused and lost, I was only finished with one phase of my life and looking for new challenges. What's next now that I've spent 30 years making people laugh? Who knows, maybe I'll lead a church or teach in a school. Maybe I'll just hike across the country. I'm not sure what's next. The one thing I do know is that I've enjoyed the ride to the fullest. I've played the hand that was dealt to me and I wouldn't trade it in for new cards.

Even with the heartache and failures, I've come to the conclusion you can't have success without them. They go hand in hand. Falling down is a part of the beginning stages of walking. Watching a baby learn to walk is central to the building blocks of learning how to fall and get back up again. I've learned from each one and it helped shape my thoughts. Even if I didn't have all the answers, I convinced myself that I did.

I do know this, from my walk down Mount Everest my senses where sharper, my vision was clearer and my ears were wide open. When the Holy Spirit spoke to me I was able to hear. When I met my current wife Jeanette Karen Peterson, I asked her one question, when you become my wife, what will your new last name be? She said Jeanette Karen Johnson. No hyphen, no middle former name. I knew we could become one. She gave me back my purpose and allowed me to stand again. I'm thankful for her gentleness and her long suffering. She put all her eggs in my basket and I try every day not to break them. When a man finds a wife he finds a good thing. I found mine and together we stand as one.

Thanks for reading my book and be on the lookout for my next book of experiences when I turn 75. God is the solution to your situation and if He's not the solution, then you have a serious situation. Until then, ENJOY LIFE!!!

Contact Information

Comedy Bookings: Call Rodney Johnson at 404.427.1056. comedianrj@aol.com (That's right. AOL.)

Motivational Speaking and Lectures: Call Kelly Cole, Prime Time Marketing at 276.591.7427.

College Appearances: Call Brian Dennis, Diversity Talent Agency at 404.539.3934.

Made in the USA
Columbia, SC
15 October 2022